C. Rzepka
41 Coles Ave., Ajax
905- 686- 8219

THE WHOLE
CHRISTMAS
CATALOGUE FOR
KiDS

THE WHOLE CHRISTMAS CATALOGUE FOR KiDS

LOUISE BETTS EGAN

LINE ILLUSTRATIONS BY KENNETH SPENGLER

PRICE STERN SLOAN
Los Angeles

A TERN BOOK

Published by Price Stern Sloan, Inc., 360 North La Cienega Boulevard, Los Angeles, California 90048

Library of Congress Cataloging-in-Publication Data

Egan, Louise.
The whole Christmas catalogue for kids / by Louise Egan. p. cm.
Summary: Explains the significance of the Christmas holiday and its traditions and provides instructions for making ornaments, decorations, gifts, cards, and goodies.

ISBN: 0-89586-741-9

1. Christmas—Juvenile literature. 2. Christmas decorations—Juvenile literature. [1. Christmas. 2. Christmas decorations.] I. Title.

GT4985.5.E35 1988   88–4140
394.2′ 6828—dc19   CIP
                    AC

THE WHOLE CHRISTMAS CATALOGUE FOR KIDS
was prepared and produced by
Tern Enterprises, Inc.
15 West 26th Street
New York, New York 10010

Editor: Nancy Kalish
Copy Editor: Patty O'Connell
Art Director/Designer: Rod L. Gonzalez
Photo Editor: Christopher Bain
Production Manager: Karen L. Greenberg

Typeset by B.P.E. Graphics
Color separations by Hong Kong Scanner Craft Company Ltd.
Printed and bound in Hong Kong

DEDICATION
To Bob and Emily, who help keep Christmas in my heart all year long.

ACKNOWLEDGMENTS
The author would like to thank Mary Cole and other staff members at The Central Children's Room of the Donnell Library Center, New York Public Library, for their gracious assistance in providing source materials for this book. Thanks also to Dr. and Mrs. Martin Pope of the Ezra Jack Keats Foundation, Inc., which provided the photograph of the homemade book *The Ugly Duckling* on page 59 by Dorothy Steuhmke. Thanks also to Karla Olson, Nancy Kalish, and Patty O'Connell for their friendly advice and sharp editing; and to Janet Basilone for her culinary guidance.

C O N T E N T S

INTRODUCTION 8

CONTENTS

PART III:

CELEBRATING CHRISTMAS 116
Favorite Stories and Carols

INTRODUCTION

When you think of Christmas, what comes to your mind? Your thoughts probably include Christmas trees, Santa Claus, presents, and wonderful smells coming from the kitchen. You may also think of singing Christmas carols, seeing pretty lights and wreaths, and going to church on Christmas Eve. There may be something else, too—a feeling that you remember, but cannot describe, a good, warm feeling mixed with excitement.

Christmas is the time of year that brings you together with family and friends. It is also a time of surprises, with beautifully wrapped presents under the tree and the mystery of Santa Claus's visit on Christmas Eve.

And Christmas is also the time of year when many people celebrate the birth of Jesus Christ. According to the Bible, it is He who spread love, peace, and hope throughout the world. He taught people to be kind to their family, friends, and neighbors and to have faith in God. During the Christmas season, people remind themselves of Jesus' message and celebrate it.

There are many things that go into making Christmas the most joyful and special time of the year. Some of them were mentioned above, but there is much, much more.

This book will help you better understand all you know about Christmas. The first section, *What Christmas Means*, tells the story of the first Christmas and many of the Christmas traditions that have developed since then, from decorating Christmas trees to waiting for Santa Claus to come down the chimney.

Robert Gray

The next section, *Holiday Crafts and Recipes,* gives instructions for making your own Christmas ornaments, decorations, and gifts. You will also learn how to wrap your gifts and create your own Christmas cards and Advent calendar. And if you want to make some Christmas goodies of your own, there are plenty of simple and delicious recipes.

The last section, *Celebrating Christmas,* includes both Christmas carols for singing and stories for reading that can be enjoyed by you and your family year after year.

Merry Christmas!

Part I

WHAT CHRISTMAS MEANS

North Wind Picture Archives

THE FIRST CHRISTMAS

The Prophecy

Long, long ago, God looked down from Heaven and saw that His world was filled with trouble. People fought each other; some people were sick; others were poor and never had enough to eat. God saw that not enough people were obeying His laws. He decided to create a son, a man who would not only help save the world from misery, but add to its glory.

"I will call my son, 'Jesus,'" God told the angels in Heaven. This name means, "God saves."

Then, God went down to earth and whispered His plan to a good and honest man named Isaiah, who lived in Judea, which is now Israel. At that time, Judea was an unhappy land. Its people, the Jews, were ruled by the cruel Romans. Isaiah rejoiced when God told him that a Savior was coming to save his people.

God told Isaiah that this Savior would be the new King, but not the sort of king that ruled the land and led armies. Instead, Jesus would lead people to a better life through faith in the Lord.

Isaiah spread God's word. People called Isaiah a "prophet" because of his prediction about the future Savior. Isaiah told the people about Jesus, saying, "His name shall be called Wonderful, Counsellor, The Mighty God, The Everlasting Father, The Prince of Peace."

A Child Is Born In Bethlehem

Mary was a pure and humble maiden, and Joseph was a good and honest man. They lived in Nazareth, a city in Galilee. God loved Mary and Joseph for their goodness and made a special plan for them.

One day, while Mary was alone at home, the angel Gabriel appeared before her. Mary was frightened at first, but Gabriel said, "Do not be afraid, for the Lord thinks highly of you. You shall be the mother of the Lord's son. The Child will be great, and his name will be 'Jesus.' "

Shortly after that, Mary and Joseph were married. It was then that Mary told Joseph that the angel Gabriel had told her that she would be the mother of the son of God. At first, Joseph did not believe it. But that night, the angel of the Lord came and told Joseph that it was true: Mary was to deliver the son of God and Joseph was to be the Child's father. Now Mary and Joseph could be glad together.

Months passed, and the time for the Child to be born was near. At the same time, the mean and greedy Roman ruler, Caesar Augustus, made a law that forced every man in Judea to return immediately to the place where he had been born. There, the people were to register their names and property, so that the ruler could collect money from them. Because Joseph had been born in Bethlehem, he and Mary were ordered to go there.

The journey from Nazareth to Bethlehem was long and hard. Joseph walked on foot, leading Mary on their donkey. After several days, they came to Bethlehem and stopped at an inn where they hoped to spend the night. "I'm sorry," said the owner, "but there's no room at the inn."

Mary and Joseph turned away, but the man saw that Mary was going to have a baby and he offered to help. "You can stay in the stable," he suggested. Mary and Joseph were grateful for any shelter, and the stable was warm and dry.

That night, which we now call Christmas Eve, Mary gave birth to a little baby boy. To keep him warm, she wrapped him tightly in strips of linen. Joseph made a cradle for the Child by spreading clean hay in the box from which the sheep ate.

Mary and Joseph were filled with joy and wonder. Jesus Christ the Savior had been born!

The Shepherds Hear The News

On the night that Jesus was born there were shepherds in a nearby field keeping watch over their flocks. Suddenly, the sky filled with light. The angel of the Lord appeared and the shepherds trembled in fear.

"Don't be afraid," said the angel, "for I have great news. Today, in the city of Bethlehem, a Child was born who is Christ the King. You shall find this Child wrapped in swaddling clothes, lying in a manger."

When the angel finished speaking, a multitude of angels appeared in the sky. "Glory to God in the highest!" they sang. "Peace on earth and good will toward men!"

After the angels had gone, the shepherds hurried to Bethlehem. There, they found Mary and Joseph sitting near the Baby Jesus, who was lying in the manger.

"An angel told us about the newborn King," said the shepherds. "May we see Him?"

Mary smiled and nodded. Joseph led the shepherds to the manger. They bowed down and thanked God for sending them the Savior, who would bring joy and hope into their lives.

The Three Wise Men

Far away in the East three wise men gazed at a strange star in the night sky. These men, who are also known as the three kings or "Magi," had never seen this star before and marveled at how much brighter it was than all the other stars.

"It must have special meaning," said one wise man.

"Perhaps it is a sign from God," said another.

The third wise man, thinking of the prophecy of Isaiah, said, "Maybe it is God's sign that our Savior has been born."

Later that night, the wise men set out on camels and rode across the desert toward the bright star. Eventually, they came to Jerusalem, where they stopped at the palace of Herod, King of Judea.

"Where can we find the newborn Baby who will be our new King?" they asked Herod. "We have seen his star in the east and have come to worship him."

King Herod had not heard anything at all about the Baby Jesus, and was troubled by the news. He called together his chief priests and scribes and asked where this Child was born.

"The prophet said that the Child will be born in Bethlehem," they replied.

King Herod then told the three wise men to continue on their way and to come back and tell him when they had found the Christ Child. "Then I can go and worship him, too," said King Herod. But the king did not mean what he said.

What the wise men did not know was that King Herod was an evil man and jealous of anyone more powerful than he. It worried him when the wise men and priests said that a new "king" had been born. King Herod wanted to be the only king in the land.

North Wind Picture Archives

The three wise men left the palace and continued following the star, which shone brightly over Bethlehem. The star led them right to Mary, Joseph, and the Baby Jesus. When they saw Jesus, the wise men fell to their knees in worship. They then opened the treasure boxes they had brought the Christ Child. Inside were gifts of gold, and frankincense and myrrh, which were precious perfumes.

The wise men were happy to have seen the Baby Jesus and looked forward to telling King Herod that they had found him. But that night, they each had a dream that warned them against telling King Herod, for fear that he would harm Jesus. The next day, the three wise men headed back to their land by another way, instead of going through Jerusalem to tell King Herod.

Jesus was safe. He would grow up and teach others to spread the word of God to as many people as possible. And the message of Jesus continues today.

Robert Gray

KEEPING THE SPIRIT OF CHRISTMAS TODAY

The Christmas spirit is what makes you feel good when you do something nice for someone. The Christmas spirit helps you feel happy on an ordinary day. That same spirit settles fights between enemies and turns misfortunes into blessings.

The Christmas spirit is something to keep inside you all year round, not just during the month of December. People refresh and renew this spirit on Christmas Day and the weeks surrounding it by continuing customs and family traditions that have been passed on through the years. Here are some of the things people do:

● **Place a star or an angel on top of the Christmas tree.** The star reminds people of the star of Bethlehem that led the three wise men to Jesus. The angel reminds people of the angel Gabriel who told Mary she would be the mother of God's son, and the angel who told the shepherds the news of Jesus' birth.

● **Sing Christmas carols.** A "carol" is a joyous song, especially about Christmas. Many of the older carols, like *Away In A Manger, The First Noël,* and *We Three Kings* tell about the birth of Christ. In a way, they are Christmas stories set to music. Other carols, like *O Christmas Tree!* and *We Wish You A Merry Christmas* bring out the more festive mood of Christmas, which makes the season extra busy and happy.

Around Christmas time, carols are sung in many places besides church. They are often sung in school, as well as played in stores and on the radio and television.

It's fun to go "Christmas caroling." Groups of friends both large and small can often be heard singing carols from house to house in the evenings. Sometimes caroling groups bring a special cheer by singing at nursing homes and hospitals.

● **Set Up A Crèche.** A "crèche," an old French word meaning "crib" or "manger," is a model of the Nativity scene, reminding people of the night Jesus was born. Inside a model stable are the figures of Mary and Joseph looking at the Baby Jesus lying in the manger. They are usually surrounded by figures of the shepherds and their sheep, and the three wise men with their camels.

In some towns, large crèches are put up in the middle of town. Many people also have small crèches in their homes.

Robert Gray

Robert Gray

Tony Cenicola

● **Exchange Gifts With Friends and Family.** Though people gave each other gifts long before Christ was born, giving and receiving presents at Christmas is a reminder of the gifts the three wise men and others gave Jesus. Giving gifts is also a way to feel the Christmas spirit, because you are doing something nice for someone else.

● **Give Money or Gifts To Others In Need.** During the holiday season, many collections are taken up for different people: for the poor, the sick, and the hungry. You may also hear or read about other needy people: perhaps a family's house has burned down, and they need clothes and shelter.

To help distribute money and gifts to these people, newspapers often have charity drives.

In many cities, members of the Salvation Army or other charities stand on street corners, ringing bells and sometimes playing hymns with horns and trumpets, encouraging passers-by to give money to the poor. Schools and offices often take up collections of toys to give to poor children. Hospitals also collect toys to give to sick children who can't be home for Christmas.

In England, Australia, and Canada, December 26 is called "Boxing Day." This is traditionally the day when people give presents or money to employees and servants. The day is named after the little clay boxes in which the money was given in medieval days. Later, wealthy people used to put their Christmas feast leftovers in boxes and give them to their servants.

Robert Gray

● **Go To Church On Christmas Eve or Christmas Day.** For many people, going to church on those days helps bring the meaning of Christmas right to the heart. Christmas carols are sung. The chapters in the Bible describing the Nativity are read, and sometimes children put on a pageant that also recalls the night Jesus was born. Many churches are decorated with candles and wreaths. The church choirs, which usually have been practicing for weeks, can sound magical at a Christmas service. For many, church is the one quiet moment among a flurry of holiday activities when it's possible to remember most clearly what Christmas is all about.

Robert Gray

CHRISTMAS GREENS

Before There Was Christmas

Thousands of years ago, and long before Christ was born, people did not understand what caused winter. Winter frightened them. They believed that the gods who watched over the crops and harvests during the spring, summer, and autumn had suddenly departed. Without these gods, there would be no more food. The gods' disappearance seemed to explain why plants died and trees grew bare; why the grass turned brown and the ground froze; and why the wind turned sharp and icy.

Daylight grew shorter and shorter, especially in Northern Europe, where snow also fell thick and deep. The fear that the sun might not return made people nervous and unhappy.

To cheer themselves up and to encourage the gods to return to earth, people all over Europe held huge festivals at the end of December. These festivals were times of great merrymaking for all. There were enormous feasts and bonfires. Houses and festival halls were decorated in evergreen branches, holly, and ivy.

Keith Glasgow

© Roz Joseph/Omni-Photo Communications

Evergreen Magic

In those ancient times, any plant that stayed green during the cold winter was thought to have magical powers. For that reason, people sometimes wore crowns of ivy and laurel around their heads. Others would drape the vines about their homes. People also would gather branches of fir, spruce, pine, and hemlock from the large evergreen forests and decorate their homes with them. The sight of all this greenery gave people hope that the other seasons would soon return. These traditions are still carried on during the Christmas holidays today, but mostly because they add to the wonderful and fun spirit of the season.

Mistletoe

This Christmas plant, which grows on a vine, was once thought to have special healing powers. It has thickly clustered leaves and tiny, white berries. People thought mistletoe was magic because its vine did not grow up from the ground. Instead, it seemed to start from nowhere and just wrap itself around tree trunks and branches.

What these people did not know was that birds ate the mistletoe berries and would then spit out the seeds. The seeds would fall into the tree bark and plant themselves there.

Ancient, mystical priests called "druids" would dress in long, hooded robes and go into the forests to cut the magical mistletoe for their religious ceremonies. They took great care to make sure the plant never touched the ground. If it did, the druids believed the mistletoe would lose its magic.

Today, mistletoe is hung from the ceilings in many homes in Great Britain and North America during the Christmas season. Any young girl or woman who stands beneath it is supposed to receive a kiss. This custom began with the ancient pagan Britons, who hung a sprig of mistletoe above their doors to scare away witches. Anyone who entered the doorway was quickly given a kiss.

When Christianity came to Great Britain, the church did not accept any of the pagan beliefs attached to the mistletoe. Though other evergreens were acceptable, mistletoe was not.

At Christmas time today, churches often light advent wreaths and decorate with evergreen branches. But if you look for mistletoe, you probably won't find it.

A gatherer brings mistletoe to market.

Holly

Like mistletoe, holly was once believed to have special magical powers that frightened off witches and other evil spirits. In England the druids wore a sprig of holly on their robes whenever they went into the forest to cut some mistletoe. They believed the holly protected them from evil spirits. Such spirits could force them to drop the mistletoe onto the ground and destroy the plant's powers.

Holly has green, glossy leaves and bright red berries. Though these berries are poisonous, they are so pretty and bright that holly has come to be a sign of cheer and plenty.

It is said that the crown of thorns that Jesus wore was made of holly. At that time, holly berries were white. But as the prickly crown pressed deeply into Jesus' forehead, his blood stained the berries. From then on, holly berries have remained red as a reminder of Jesus' suffering for all people.

Brilliant poinsettias seem to shout out "Merry Christmas!"

The Poinsettia

The Mexicans first called this plant, "Flower of the Holy Night," because of the way its top cluster of green leaves mysteriously turns red in December. The poinsettia grows wild in Mexico and was brought to the United States in the 1830s by a congressman and botanist named Joel Roberts Poinsett. The plant was named after him. To Poinsett, the plant's pretty red leaves resembled a bright star, whose center was lit with a bright, yellow blossom.

There is a legend that tells of a little Mexican boy who wished to give a present to the Christ Child. But the boy was poor and had no present to give Him. One Christmas Eve, he stood outside the church while everyone else went inside bearing their special gifts. The little boy was too ashamed to go inside with nothing to offer.

"At least I can pray," the boy thought to himself. He walked over to the window from where the church music could best be heard, and knelt down. The little boy then closed his eyes, put his hands together, and prayed. When the music ended, he said, "Amen," and stood up. To his amazement, a beautiful plant had grown in the spot where he had knelt. The plant had flaming red leaves arranged like a star, and a lovely yellow blossom shone like a light in the center.

The little boy realized that this flower was a gift from God. He gently plucked it and then carried it into the church. Everyone looked on happily as the boy proudly laid his gift at the altar.

© Craig Blouin/Manhattan Views Inc.

CHRISTMAS TREES

The Legend of the First Christmas Tree

As the newborn Christ Child lay in His manger, shepherds, wise men, and even birds and beasts came to the stable to offer the new Savior gifts. In the corner of the stable stood a sad little fir tree. The tree had seen many of the gifts and thought they were all splendid. There were both fancy and simple gifts. The little tree also wanted to give something to the newborn Savior, and he was sad because he thought he had nothing that the Baby Jesus would want.

"All I have to offer the Christ Child are my needles, and they will only prick Him," he thought. "They are not right at all!" And the little fir bowed his head in shame.

Looking down from Heaven, God saw how disappointed the tree was. Quietly, God called out to the stars and said, "Please go down and rest on the branches of the little fir tree who so dearly wishes to please the Baby Jesus."

The stars gladly obeyed. They fell from the night sky like little drops of silver and came to rest on the tree's branches. Soon, the little fir was covered with a brilliant glow!

The Christ Child looked up at the tree and smiled. He then stretched out His arms to touch the beautiful branches. The little fir tree glowed even brighter when he saw how he pleased the Infant.

Each year after that, people were said to put candles or lights on Christmas trees to remind one another how the little tree's starlights delighted the Baby Jesus.

Robert Gray

Robert Gray

Since it is illegal in many places to cut your own tree, Christmas tree farms, like the one on the left, were started to meet the growing demand for trees during this season. Two of the most popular types of tree are the umbrella pine (top left) and the red pine (top right). This beautiful frosted conifer (right) helps us see what the first Christmas tree might have looked like.

© John Gerlach/Tom Stack & Associates

© Peter Poulides/Manhattan Views Inc.

The Christmas Tree Tradition

Today Christmas trees adorn homes all over the world during the month of December. To many, these decorated evergreen trees represent the spirit of Christmas. To others, they represent the continuation of life in the winter.

People first wrote about Christmas trees about five hundred years ago, in Germany. There, it is said, a religious man named Martin Luther was walking through the woods one starry night around Christmas time. He was so struck by the beauty of the starlight on the evergreen trees that he chopped a small tree down and brought it home for his wife and children. He lighted the tree with small candles, which he said represented Christ as the Light of the World.

The idea of Christmas trees began to spread throughout Northern Europe, where evergreen trees grow tall and strong. Even so, the first Christmas trees—like Martin Luther's—were small enough to display on a table. Family members would put their gifts on the table underneath the little tree. The trees were decorated with bright paper roses, glass ornaments, apples, cookies, and candies. Small lighted candles were then carefully placed at the ends of the branches. (A bucket of water was usually kept nearby, in case one of the candles accidentally dropped onto a branch.)

When Germans came over to the United States in the 1800s, they brought the Christmas tree tradition with them. Other early Americans liked this tradition and quickly adopted it. No longer were Christmas trees small enough for tables. They would go out to the forest and chop down the tallest, most magnificent tree they saw. Most of them were several feet high, and many touched the ceiling.

As pioneers headed west, they did not always have bright and pretty decorations for their trees. Instead, they made little ornaments from materials gathered in the field and forest, such as acorns, nuts, corn shucks, hay, sticks, wood pieces, pine cones, and wild berries. People also hung gingerbread and sugar cookies, as well as garlands of popcorn and cranberries. Though these trees may not have been the most colorful, the love and spirit that went into making the ornaments was enough to make the smallest tree look grand.

Tree-trimming Advice

Today many families decorate their Christmas trees with both handmade and store-bought ornaments. Sometimes people collect ornaments on vacations. Over the years, many ornaments begin to mean something special to each family. Taking the pretty family decorations out of their boxes often gives people a warm, good feeling. It adds to the joy of seeing the family tree trimmed to its very best.

Sometimes people disagree about which ornament would look best where. Because decorating the tree is a shared activity, it's best to listen to one another's ideas; keep in mind that your tree will look good wherever you put the ornament.

However, it's best to put delicate ornaments high up, on strong branches where they are least likely to get knocked off. You may need to use a stepladder, so make sure an adult is watching you.

The lower branches are the ones people and pets bump into most often. For that reason, sturdy, unbreakable ornaments should go on the lower branches. That way, if an ornament does get knocked off, it won't break.

The Christmas tree at Rockefeller Center in New York City enchants all who come to see it. Nearby, on Fifth Avenue (right), holiday lights sparkle, invoking the spirit of the season.

Favorite Christmas Trees

Many large cities are known for their giant Christmas trees. These trees are visited by thousands of children and adults every year.

Some of these trees are made up of hundreds of normal-sized Christmas trees that have been tied together to make them several stories high. They are then covered in brilliant lights and ornaments. One such "tree" is in Chicago, inside Marshall Field's department store. It attracts many hundreds of children and adults each year.

Other cities put up a single, but larger than average, Christmas tree. Washington, D.C.'s Christmas tree, located near the White House, is decorated with fifty large, brightly colored balls that represent each state. Another enormous tree is in New York City, at Rockefeller Center, where it towers over an outdoor skating rink. In London, a giant tree stands in Trafalgar Square. The Norwegians send this tree every year, to thank the British for their help to Norway during World War II.

Of course, the large and famous Christmas trees may not be everyone's favorite. Sometimes, the Christmas tree that lights up your own town square may seem to be the most beautiful tree of all.

Robert Gray

CHRISTMAS LIGHTS

At Christmas time, lights seem to go up everywhere. Whole avenues are lit with small white lights that glisten like fairies. Strings of colored lights brighten neighborhood lawns and storefronts, and cheery Christmas tree lights glow from inside homes.

Lights have long been a part of the Christmas tradition. The bright light from the Star of Bethlehem guided the three wise men to the Baby Jesus. Later, Jesus said to the Twelve Apostles, "Let your light so shine before men." He called these apostles "the light of the world."

The "light" Jesus meant was a spiritual one. He wanted his disciples to do their very best and to be an example to others. To this day, Christmas is a time when people remember those words through giving presents, good behavior, and acts of kindness.

Churches light candles to recall the light that came to the world with the birth of Jesus Christ. The Advent wreath is one way of representing the spirit of Christmas: Four candles are placed around a wreath and a new candle is lit each of the four Sundays of the Advent season, prior to Christmas day. On Christmas Eve, churches also hold special candlelight services.

A custom in many European homes is to place a candle in the window to light the way for the Christ Child's coming each December 25.

In the American Southwest, "luminarias," or Christmas lanterns, are a popular tradition. These lanterns are made by setting a small candle in a paper bag that is weighted down with moist sand. Sometimes whole neighborhoods mark their driveways with luminarias, and the sight of hundreds of these glowing lanterns is splendid.

December is the coldest and darkest month of the year for many countries that celebrate Christmas. For that reason, lights are all the more important in adding cheer and warmth throughout the holidays.

Color and lights create a special kind of magic at Christmas. The Lucia Queen (right), with a candle wreath on top of her head, brings a special Christmas breakfast to her family.

New York Public Library/Picture Collection

Customs With Candles—Caution!

Never attempt to make your own Christmas decoration that involves lighting candles or matches, unless you have *an adult's permission.* These decorations are beautiful when lit, but they can also be *dangerous* if the candle happens to fall over and catch fire. For that reason, it's important for an adult to supervise any candle lighting.

St. Lucia Day—The Swedish Tribute to Light

Sweden's "Lucia Festival," on December 13, is held at a time when darkness falls in that country by mid-afternoon. The name Lucia, or Lucy, means "light," which is something Swedes especially treasure during the long winter nights.

The real Lucia was a kind and courageous Christian woman who lived in Italy in the fourth century. It is said that on the night before her wedding, Lucia gave all her money to the poor. Because no one could understand why she did that, Lucia was accused of being a witch and was burned at the stake on December 13 in the year 304. Even after her death, however, Lucia was said to continue helping those in need. For that reason, she was eventually made a saint.

When Christianity came to Sweden, St. Lucia's role was combined with that of Berchta, the early goddess of the hearth, or fireplace. This goddess was loved for her good heart and for the special care she was said to give to children.

According to Swedish tradition, the oldest daughter of the family pretends to be St. Lucia on the morning of December 13. The "Lucia Queen" dresses in a long white gown and wears a special crown of evergreen boughs and four lighted candles upon her head. She rises before dawn to prepare coffee and special saffron buns and then serves them to the rest of the family, while they are still in bed.

As she goes from room to room, the Lucia Queen sings a song of promise that the darkness will end soon. The sight of this Lucia Queen, with the candles burning brightly on her evergreen crown, is one that brings hope, light, and happiness to all.

Robert Gray

SPECIAL CHRISTMAS WORDS

Advent is a season during the church year that begins on the last Sunday in November and ends on Christmas. "Advent" means "the coming of Jesus Christ." For many people, Advent is the time for improving one's thoughts and behavior, in preparation for Christmas. The color purple symbolizes Advent and you may notice its use in church during those weeks. Advent calendars and Advent wreaths are both good and fun ways to mark the coming of Christmas.

Christmas Seals. By the early 1900s Christmas cards had become popular and tons of Christmas mail overwhelmed post offices around the world. About that time, a young postal clerk in Denmark named Einar Holboell thought of using Christmas cards as a way to raise money for a good cause. He wanted to help the many people, especially children, who at that time were suffering and dying from the crippling disease tuberculosis.

Holboell looked at the hundreds of thousands of letters, parcels, and Christmas cards that swamped his post office. He thought that if each piece of mail carried an extra stamp that cost only a penny, the money could go toward building more hospitals and to treating tuberculosis.

Holboell talked about this idea to everyone he met and found that people were interested. Finally, even the Danish King Christian expressed his approval.

The first Christmas seal stamp came out in Denmark in 1904 and four million were sold. A Danish immigrant, Jacob Riis, who later became a famous journalist, photographer, and reformer, introduced the idea to the United States. The double-barred Cross of Lorraine became the seal's emblem in 1919.

In the 1920s, the selling of Christmas seals was taken over by the National Tuberculosis Association, now called the American Lung Association. By the time

Einar Holboell died in 1927, he had received many honors, including knighthood. But what probably pleased him most was the progress and success in fighting tuberculosis.

Today, more than forty countries issue Christmas seals. In the United States, the American Lung Association sends Christmas seals to people through the mail and asks for a contribution. Thanks largely to the money raised from this effort, tuberculosis has become a rare disease in most advanced nations.

Epiphany (see *Twelve Days of Christmas*)

Figgy Pudding. Anyone who has ever sung the British Christmas carol, "We Wish You A Merry Christmas," has probably wondered about the second verse, which says, "We all want some figgy pudding...so bring it right here!" This dessert was made from figs and raisins, and it was popular among British seamen during the nineteenth century.

Today, figgy pudding is largely unheard of in Great Britain. (There, the special "Christmas pudding" is made from plums, a Christmas tradition that is centuries old.) A recipe for fig pudding in the cookbook, *Joy of Cooking,* suggests that this dessert is more of a sweet bread or cake than what Americans would consider "pudding."

Frankincense and Myrrh, two of the gifts the three wise men gave the Baby Jesus are pleasant smelling substances made from the sap of certain trees found in Northeast Africa. At the time when Jesus was born, these types of incense were difficult to obtain and considered very valuable.

Good King Wenceslas (pronounced: Wen-suss-luss) is the name and subject of an

Courtesy American Lung Association

English Christmas carol. This carol is based on a legend about King Wenceslas of Bohemia, a land that was once part of western Czechoslovakia. Wenceslas reigned during the tenth century and did much to strengthen people's belief in Christianity. He was known for his generosity and kindness. By the beginning of the next century, Wenceslas had become the patron saint of Bohemia.

The carol "Good King Wenceslas" tells the story of how one bitterly cold night on the Feast of St. Stephen (December 26), King Wenceslas looked out his castle window. Outside, the moonlight shone on the deep, crusty snow, and he saw a peasant gathering firewood. The king felt sorry for the poor man and called one of his pages to find out where the peasant lived. When the page replied that the peasant lived far away, the king called for some meat, wine, and firewood, which he decided he and the page would bring to the man's house.

The journey to the peasant's house was long, cold, and difficult in the deep snow. Finally, the page said that he was too cold to go any further. But King Wenceslas told the page that if he followed along in the king's footprints, he would feel warmer. The servant obeyed and, miraculously, heat seemed to come out of each of King Wenceslas's footsteps. The carol's lesson is, "Those that help the poor shall be helped as well."

Jesus, or Jesus Christ is the name that people call the Son of God, who is hon-ored on Christmas. In the Bible, Mary is told that she will name her son, "Jesus." This is the Greek name for "Joshua," which means "Savior" in Hebrew, the original language of the Bible. The name, "Christ," is a Greek word that means, "Messiah," or "Holy One."

Manger, the place where Mary placed the Baby Jesus upon his birth, is a trough or open box in which food for cattle, horses, or sheep is placed. It is probable that Mary's husband, Joseph, cleaned the manger and spread it with fresh hay, before laying his newborn son in it.

Noël is the French word for "Christmas." The Christmas carol "The First Noël"

Shepherds visit the Baby Jesus on the first Noel.

(sometimes spelled "Nowell") has made it a familiar word to English-speaking countries as well. "Noël" is derived from the Latin words for "birthday" ("Dies Natalis"), for it is on Christmas that people celebrate the Birth of Christ. In Italy, Christmas is called "Il Natale;" in Portugal and Brazil, "O Natal;" in Spanish-speaking countries, "La Navidad;" and in Wales, "Nadolig."

Swaddling clothes. In olden times, newborn babies were wrapped tightly in strips of linen or other cloth. This made them feel warm, secure, and protected. The word "swaddling" comes from an Old English word meaning "to wrap."

Twelve Days of Christmas. The twelve days from Christmas to Epiphany, on January 6, were once considered sacred.

In ancient Eastern Europe, Christians thought celebrating one's birthday—even the Birth of Christ—was unholy. For that reason, Eastern Christians used to celebrate Epiphany, which is also called "Little Christmas" and "Twelfth Day." Epiphany commemorates the three wise men's arrival in Bethlehem, which was a sign to all that Jesus was truly the Son of God.

Nothing invokes the spirit of the Christmas season more than stockings hung by the fireplace.

Yule is another name for the Christmas season of festivity and feasting. The word comes from ancient times, before Christ, when people in Northern Europe held their mid-winter festivals. "Yule" is thought to come from the ancient word for "wheel," which referred to the sun. This mid-winter "Yuletide" season was when people prayed to their gods for the sun and warmth to return to earth.

Yule Log Burning the Yule log is a tradition that was passed down from ancient Scandinavia. Though this custom was once practiced widely throughout Europe, it is now known mainly in England.

"Bringing in the Yule log" meant finding and cutting down a large tree on Christmas Eve. The log had to be very large, for it was supposed to burn throughout the twelve days of Christmas. Giant oak trees with large, twisted roots were often good choices.

Getting the log home was a group activity and especially fun for children. The log was tied up in a rope, and everyone who helped pull the log home was said to have good luck in the coming year. The log would be placed on the hearth, or fireplace, and lit with some of the kindling from last year's log.

Scraps from Yule logs were put away carefully each year after the holiday, to be taken out to light the next year's Yule log. In the meantime, people believed that the wood pieces would protect their home from fire and lightning during the year ahead.

Wassail (pronounced: WASS-el or was-SALE) means "to your health!" It is an ancient English toast that was usually said during festive celebrations. People would raise their glasses of wine, shout out "Wassail!" and then drink, as a sign of goodwill to each other.

"Wassail" is also a drink made from ale or wine, or both, and spiced with roasted apples and sugar. The bowl in which it is served is called a "wassail bowl."

"Wassailing" refers to the revelry that usually occurs while drinking from the wassail bowl.

THE STORY OF SANTA CLAUS AND OTHER SPECIAL CHRISTMAS PEOPLE

Who has a long, white beard, wears a bright, red suit and stocking cap, and brings presents and joy to children at Christmas? Why, Santa Claus, of course! All over the world, children of all ages look forward to Santa's yearly visit, for Santa Claus, or "Father Christmas," as he is known in some countries, is everybody's special friend.

And yet Santa is a mystery—a sort of magical mystery. After all, very few people (if any) have actually seen Santa Claus deliver presents on Christmas Eve. Santa only visits homes once everyone is asleep.

Still, most people agree that Santa rides through the sky on a sleigh pulled by reindeer. They also agree that Santa slips down the chimney (or enters the house in some other mysterious way, if there is no chimney), fills children's stockings with little gifts and goodies, and leaves bigger presents around the Christmas tree.

Santa Claus is known to live at the North Pole, where he, Mrs. Claus, and his troop of merry elves work all year making presents for good girls and boys. Throughout the year, Santa receives many, many letters from children, who tell Santa what they would like for Christmas. Santa usually does his best to give children what they want.

On Christmas Eve, he loads up his sleigh with sacks of toys and harnesses his team of flying reindeer to it. Then, with a "Ho! Ho! Ho!", Santa climbs into the sleigh and flies off into the night, delivering presents to children around the world.

The next morning, the signs that Santa Claus has visited are usually clear: the

Who Was Saint Nicholas?

Santa Claus is really a shortened name for Saint Nicholas. This saint lived almost two thousand years ago in Asia Minor, which is now the country Turkey. He was not born a saint, but rather, just a simple, good boy named Nicholas.

When Nicholas grew up, he became a bishop and spread the word of Christ. At that time, Christianity was not accepted by most people, including the evil ruler of Asia Minor. Bishop Nicholas and his Christian followers were thrown in prison for their beliefs. But Nicholas was brave and helped encourage his fellow prisoners to be strong. Finally, after seven long years in prison, a new, kind ruler came to power and set Nicholas and the other Christians free.

The years that Nicholas had spent in prison had made him wiser, more understanding, and more willing than ever to help others. By the time he died, on December 6 in the year 343, there were many stories about his good deeds.

These tales were such fine examples of faith, courage, and kindness, that the memory of the good Bishop Nicholas lived on in people's hearts. Soon, he was declared a saint. As years passed, the legends about St. Nicholas grew. He became known as the Secret Gift-Bringer, as well as the Protector of Children.

snack that was laid out for him is eaten, he has left his gifts and perhaps a note for the children of the house, and *sometimes* it's even possible to see sleigh tracks on the roof!

But where did Santa Claus come from? How old is he? Has he always been magical? These are difficult questions, especially since no one was around when Santa Claus was born. Nevertheless, historians have found writings and tales that help provide the answers to these questions. Some of these stories are told in the following pages.

In olden days, people believed Saint Nicholas rode a white horse to deliver his presents.

THE SECRET GIFT-BRINGER

When St. Nicholas was a young man in Asia Minor, he heard about a merchant so poor that he thought he would have to sell his three lovely daughters into slavery. The eldest daughter wished to marry, but because she had no wealth to offer a husband, no man wanted her.

Nicholas knew the merchant would be too proud to accept any money as charity, so he came up with a secret plan to save the merchant and his daughters. Late one night, Nicholas wrapped three gold coins in a cloth and crept through the dark streets to the merchant's house. When he was sure that all were asleep, Nicholas tossed the little sack of coins into the house through an open window. Then he hurried back home.

When the merchant awoke the next morning, he could not believe his eyes: there, lying in the hearth, were three gold coins. He could not imagine who would have given him such a gift, so he believed it was from God. One gold coin was all the eldest daughter needed for a wedding offer, and she was soon married. The other two daughters were able to remain at home with their father.

But when it came time for the second daughter to marry, there was no money left. Again, Nicholas crept to the house and secretly tossed more gold coins in through the window. The merchant was amazed and grateful at finding more money. He accepted the gold as a gift from God, but now he was curious.

When the youngest daughter was ready to marry, Nicholas returned to the house once more. Quietly, he tossed the coins in through the window. But this time, the merchant had been waiting and watching. He jumped up and ran out the door.

"Stop! Wait!" the merchant called, and he ran until he caught up with Nicholas.

Nicholas begged the old man not to tell anyone of his deed. The merchant reluctantly obeyed and did not tell the secret, until he was about to die. Then he told the tale, and once it became known, the story spread throughout the land and established St. Nicholas as The Secret Gift-Bringer.

THE PROTECTOR OF CHILDREN

A young fisherman's son named Basil was walking along the beach one day when, suddenly, Arab pirates sprang out from hiding and kidnapped him. The pirates brought Basil to their land and made him a servant in the emperor's palace.

Meanwhile, Basil's parents did not know what had happened to their son. They cried and cried over their loss, and every day they prayed for Basil's safe return. A year passed, and Basil was still lost. On December 6, St. Nicholas Day, Basil's parents went to church and prayed extra hard for their son to come home.

That evening, the dogs began barking furiously outside Basil's house. The two parents went to see what was wrong—and then cried out in joy: there, at the gate in servant's clothing, was their son!

Basil told them how he had been kidnapped a year before. "But tonight," he said, "as I was serving the ruler's dinner, I suddenly felt myself being lifted into the sky. I turned around and saw I was staring right into the eyes of St. Nicholas."

Basil then had looked down and was startled to see that the earth was far below him.

"Don't be afraid," St. Nicholas had said, and Basil relaxed, knowing the good saint would protect him.

"Where are you taking me?" the young boy asked.

"I'm returning you to your parents," said St. Nicholas, "because they have prayed so hard for you to come home."

Basil and his family lived happily together for many years. The story of Basil's rescue was retold everywhere, and St. Nicholas became known as the Protector of Children.

New York Public Library/Picture Collection

ST. NICHOLAS COMES TO EUROPE

The tales and legends of St. Nicholas were passed on from generation to generation over the centuries that followed. St. Nicholas was so beloved that Russia and Greece adopted him as their patron (or protector) saint, and hundreds of churches throughout Europe were dedicated to him.

December 6, the Feast of St. Nicholas, was celebrated as the time when the saint would make his annual trip to earth.

Back then, people perceived St. Nicholas as a stately, bearded bishop who wore

© K. Reinhardt 1987/FPG Intl.

long, flowing robes and rode a white horse. On his head he wore a tall, pointed bishop's hat and he carried a staff as a symbol of his power and goodness. Children especially looked forward to his visit, for St. Nicholas was their protector and a gift-bringer as well.

On the eve of St. Nicholas Day, children would set hay and carrots out on the doorstep for the saint's white horse to eat, after his long trip down to earth from Heaven. It seemed only natural that St. Nicholas would give children something in return. At first, the saint left little presents hidden inside carrots and cabbages. In time, St. Nicholas brought different kinds of gifts, and he left them in children's shoes or stockings placed by the hearth.

But even in those days, St. Nicholas was a mystery. No one could ever say for sure exactly how the saint appeared on the eve of his feast day, because no one ever saw him.

In Belgium, St. Nicholas was thought to carry a big book so he could write down the names of the good children who deserved gifts. In Holland, St. Nicholas delivered presents to the good children, while a mean-looking servant called "Black Peter" carried birch rods for the naughty ones. Black Peter also carried a big, heavy bag for carrying away extremely bad children. In Germany, a bearded man dressed all in fur, named "Fur Nicholas," carried a bag of coal with him to give to bad children.

The thought of Black Peter or Fur Nicholas would scare children into being good. But no one ever feared St. Nicholas—he rewarded the good children but never punished the bad.

ST. NICHOLAS AS FATHER CHRISTMAS

Once Christianity had been established throughout Europe, people began to have religious differences. Eventually, Christians split into two main groups: the Catholics (the older group) and the Protestants.

Protestants in England, France, and Germany stopped worshipping saints altogether—including St. Nicholas. But it was impossible to forget this good saint and protector of children. Instead, they gave St. Nicholas a new name: "Father Christmas," or "Père Nöel" in French. In parts of Switzerland and West Germany, St. Nicholas came to be called simply, "Ni-kolaus," or the "Weihnachtsman," which means "the Christmas man."

In some countries, Father Christmas continued to come on December 6, the Feast of St. Nicholas, while in others, he arrived on Christmas Eve. Otherwise, the new "Father Christmas" remained very much like the good St. Nicholas everyone had always known. Father Christmas still dressed in bishop's robes and rode a tall, white horse, and he continued to bring presents to all good children.

Over time, Father Christmas changed his style and appearance. Today, especially in Europe, Father Christmas is every inch the same "jolly old elf" whom Americans call Santa Claus, and he is loved just as much.

Gift-Bringers From Around The World

Many children around the world await different gift-bringers. Still, these gift-bringers are just as magical, mysterious, and well-loved as St. Nicholas, Santa Claus, and Father Christmas.

THE BEFANA OF ITALY

The Befana is a mysterious, old woman who visits the world on the eve of Epiphany. Some people call Befana a witch, for she has magical powers to reward good children and punish the bad ones. But throughout Italy, the Befana is known for her kind heart and for bringing goodies and gifts to children.

In some areas of Italy, the Befana announces her approach to each house by ringing a bell. That is her signal for children to go to bed, for the Befana will not enter a house until all are asleep. Many children hang stockings by the window for the Befana to fill with sweets, fruits, and gifts.

The Befana, known as the "Baboushka" in Russia, is said to have passed up the opportunity to join the three wise men on their search for the Baby Jesus. Because she never found the Christ Child herself and was not able to give him a present, the Befana began secretly bringing presents to other children instead. The Befana makes her trip each year on January 5. (For the complete story, see page 124.)

JULTOMTE: THE SWEDISH CHRISTMAS ELF

In olden days, when most people in Sweden lived on farms, people believed that goblins, trolls, and other strange creatures, called "jultomten" (pro-nounced: yool-TOME-Ten), lived in the nooks and crannies of every home. These creatures caused much mischief, especially in the cold, dark month of December. Families would try to get along with these jultomten as best they could. They would leave them porridge to eat and keep the house as clean as possible.

Over the years, the jultomten have mostly disappeared. Perhaps they are hiding in the forest and countryside. Now Swedish children are visited by the good and jolly gift-bringer, the "Jultomte," the Swedish name for Santa Claus.

In Sweden, the Jultomte does things a little differently from other countries. There, he comes on foot and carries his bag of toys and goodies on his back. The Jultomte arrives early on Christmas Eve, while the children are still awake and eagerly awaiting his arrival.

© Cathy Christy O'Connor

"Las Posadas," the traditional Spanish procession, reenacts the night Jesus was born.

As this painting by N.C. Wyeth illustrates, Santa Claus visits homes all over the world with his sack of toys.

THE THREE KINGS OF MEXICO

The Christmas season in Mexico and other Spanish-speaking countries begins with colorful parades and candlelight processions in the evening. The processions, called "Las Posadas," act out the night Jesus was born. Children dress up as angels, shepherds, Mary, Joseph, and the Three Kings.

Festivities continue through Epiphany, January 6, which is also called "Three Kings Day." This was the day the Three Kings (or wise men) found Jesus lying in the manger in Bethlehem. On Epiphany Eve, the Three Kings come down to earth, dressed in their long, royal robes and crowns. Before going to sleep on that night, children set their shoes out on the doorstep so the Three Kings may fill them with gifts and candies as they pass.

THE "LITTLE CHRIST CHILD" OF WEST GERMANY

The "Christkindl," (pronounced: Krisst KIN-del) or "Little Christ Child" looks like a young angel, dressed in white robes with golden wings and a crown. He flies down to earth on Christmas Eve, and puts presents for children under the Christmas tree.

Today, "Kriss Kringle" is another name for Santa Claus. The name came from the Germans, who brought their "Christkindl" with them when they came to the United States. Their American neighbors, who did not understand German, thought they were saying, "Kriss Kringle." In time, German-American children adopted the American Santa Claus as their Christmas gift-bearer, and Kriss Kringle and Santa Claus became one and the same.

YOU CAN BE A GIFT-BRINGER TOO

To be a gift-bringer in your own family or circle of friends, it's not necessary to dress up as one. All you need are the kind and generous thoughts of giving joy to others, which all gift-bringers share.

Presents do not have to be as fancy or expensive as the gifts the three wise men gave Jesus. Instead, think of the story of the little Mexican boy, who gave the Baby Jesus a simple poinsettia.

The following section will give you ideas on how to make your own presents, or how to add a personal touch to something you have bought. Remember: What makes each gift valuable is the thought and love behind it.

Gift giving, inspired by the first Christmas when the three wise men brought gold, frankincense, and myrrh to the Christ Child, has become one of the hallmarks of the Christmas season.

Part II

HOLIDAY CRAFTS AND RECIPES

Richard Waldmann

HOW TO MAKE CHRISTMAS CARDS

Everyone likes to receive Christmas cards—and receiving a handmade card is even better. It means that someone has taken a little extra time, thought, and imagination to send you holiday greetings. And that's what Christmas is all about.

There is no one way to make a Christmas card; what your card looks like depends on what you like doing best. This section explains how to make six different types of cards:

Christmas drawings
Christmas card cut-outs from paper
Christmas card cut-outs from other material
Christmas sponge patterns
Christmas card cut-outs from magazines
Christmas photographs

These ideas are meant to help you decide what kind of card you wish to make. Feel free to use your imagination, however, to make your card unique.

What You Need To Make Your Christmas Card:

- Construction Paper. This paper is both sturdy and colorful. It is thick enough to support glued-on shapes, and if you draw on it with colored markers, the ink will not leak through to the other side.
- Scissors. Safety scissors, which are small, light, and easy to handle, are the best kind of scissors to use. If you must use a larger, sharper pair, make sure you have your parents' permission.
- Glue. Use regular white glue or rubber cement as an adhesive, according to the following suggestions.

A WORD ABOUT GLUES

White glue can be squeezed easily from a small, plastic bottle. It's easy to use and sticks well. However, once you have glued something, like a picture, onto your paper, it is

*Professionally made cards often can provide inspiration for your own unique Christmas
card designs.*

White glue is easy to dab on but if you make a mistake it is harder to wipe off than rubber cement.

Tony Cenicola

GLUING TIPS

1. Apply the glue evenly to whatever you wish to attach to your card. The most important areas to cover are the corners. You may want to take your finger and smear a little of the glue smoothly onto the corners and along the sides.

2. With rubber cement, wipe the excess from the brush on the side of the container before applying the brush to the item being glued on.

3. Whether using rubber cement or white glue, never apply it heavily or in big globs—the result will be messy and lumpy if you do.

4. For extra small cut-outs or corners, it sometimes helps to put a small mound of adhesive on an extra piece of paper or cardboard. Lightly dip your finger into it and dab it onto your cut-out or corner.

GLITTER TIPS

Trimming your card with glitter is easy and it adds a bit of sparkle as well. *Make sure your work space is covered with newspaper.* Here's what you do:

1. Figure out where you want the glitter to go—around the edges, in a special design, or in a particular place.

2. Brush the rubber cement or squeeze the white glue onto the place where you want the glitter.

3. Quickly, before the cement or glue dries, pour the glitter over it on the page. Put on lots of glitter so that every spot is covered.

4. Let the card dry for a few minutes.

5. Pick up the finished card and shake the extra glitter onto the newspaper. You can save that extra glitter for later projects.

almost impossible to change it without tearing the paper or leaving glue marks.

Rubber cement usually comes in a jar with a brush attached to the top. It sticks as well as white glue, but rubber cement allows you to make mistakes. In most cases, you can pull off whatever you have glued on without tearing it. Be sure to pull it off gently, though. Once you have pulled it off, simply rub off the dried glue. Then apply some fresh rubber cement, and stick the item back on the card.

How To Begin Your Christmas Card:

1. Take a piece of construction paper. Notice that it has two long sides and two short sides.

2. Bring the two short sides together at one end. Flatten the other end down to make a fold. We'll call this Fold #1.

3. Now bring the two short sides together again, and make another fold. We'll call this Fold #2.

4. With your scissors, cut along Fold #2.

5. You should now have two equal-sized cards, ready to decorate.

Fold the two short sides of the paper together. Then bring the two short sides together again.

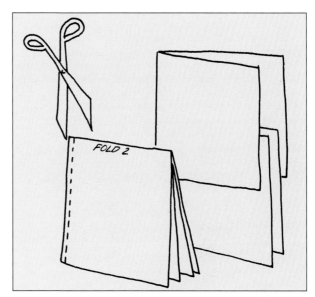

Next, cut the paper in half to create two cards.

"But What Should It Look Like?"—Ideas For Your Cards

- Think of the friend or relative who will receive your card. What do you and that person do together? What does that person like? Did you have an adventure together? Did you do something wonderful together *last* Christmas that you hope this special person will remember, too? Use your memories to help give you an idea.

- Look all around you for Christmas ideas. Is your town dressed up in wreaths and colored lights? Are there Christmas trees in your neighbors' windows and wreaths on their doors? Those make pretty pictures.

- Look at the ornaments on a Christmas tree, or the pictures on wrapping paper for ideas. Bakery shop windows often have
- gingerbread houses, gingerbread men, and Christmas cookies on display. Those make good pictures, too.
- Christmas books and magazines are also full of fun pictures. Use them for ideas.

Below are six different types of Christmas cards to make. Choose the one that will be the most fun for you to create. If you do not have two plain, equal-sized cards ready to decorate, go back to *"What You Need To Make Your Christmas Card"* and *"How To Begin Your Christmas Card"* and follow those instructions. Then continue your card-making with the directions below.

CHRISTMAS DRAWINGS

What You Need: pencil, crayons, colored markers, colored pencils or paint, white or light-colored paper.

Optional: glitter and glue.

What You Do:

1. In pencil, draw a Christmas picture on the front of your card. (It's best not to color your picture until the written message is finished, too.)

2. Once your picture is right, print a message in pencil on the inside of the card. For variety, you can start the message on the outside cover and finish it on the inside.

3. Go over your message in colored marker or crayon.

4. Now color your card.

Optional:

5. Trim your card with glitter.

CHRISTMAS CARD CUT-OUTS FROM PAPER

What You Need: pencil, construction paper or Christmas wrapping paper, scissors, glue, colored markers or crayons.

Optional: glitter.

What You Do:

1. Using a pencil, draw a Christmas shape, such as a candle, star, Christmas tree, or Christmas tree ornament, on a clean piece of colored construction paper. If you have trouble drawing, perhaps you can find an appropriate shape on Christmas wrapping paper and cut that out.

2. Carefully cut the shape out with scissors.

3. Glue it onto the front of your card.

4. Write your Christmas message on your card in pencil first, then go over it in colored marker or crayon.

Optional:

5. Trim your card with glitter.

CHRISTMAS CARD CUT-OUTS FROM OTHER MATERIAL

What You Need: small pieces of pretty material—cotton, felt, gingham, or practically any leftover material in a sewing basket (*and* permission to use the material), pencil, scissors, glue, colored markers.

Optional: glitter, cotton puffs, ribbon.

What You Do:

1. With a pencil, draw a simple Christmas shape—a candle, star, Christmas tree, or Christmas tree ornament on your piece of material.

2. Carefully cut out the pattern from the material.

3. Decide where you want the cut-out to go on your card, and then glue it in place.

4. With a pencil, write your Christmas message on your card. Go over the message with colored marker or crayon.

Optional:

5. Trim your card with glitter, different small pieces of material, ribbon, or even bits of cotton puffs for a snow effect.

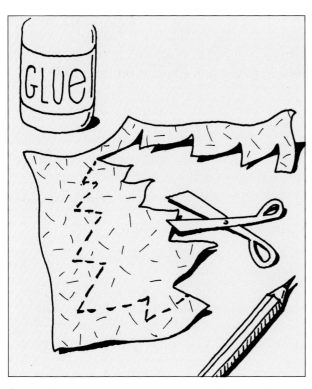

Cut your favorite Christmas shape from a pretty piece of fabric.

Glue the shape to your card and add a simple message.

© Christopher Bain 1988

Tony Cenicola

Dip your sponge piece in paint and lightly press it to the paper. You can repeat the pattern many times.

CHRISTMAS SPONGE PATTERNS

What You Need: a small sponge, scissors, poster paints, extra paper (for practice prints).

What You Do:

1. Wet the sponge, then squeeze out extra water. (Damp sponges are easier to cut than dry ones.)

2. From the sponge, cut out a single Christmas shape—such as a candle, Christmas tree, or Christmas tree ornament. You could also simply cut out small circles or triangles to make a pretty design on your card.

3. Dip one side of the sponge cut-out into paint.

4. Make a test print with the sponge cut-out on an extra piece of paper. You may need to use more paint to make a heavier print, or less paint to make it lighter.

5. Once you have the right amount of paint on your sponge cut-out, press it against the paper to make a print or design onto your Christmas card.

6. Make as many prints on your card as you wish, but save room for your message and your name.

7. Print your Christmas message in pencil, then go over it in colored marker or crayon.

CHRISTMAS CARD CUT-OUTS FROM MAGAZINES

What You Need: old magazines or old Christmas cards (*and* permission to cut pictures out of them), scissors, glue, pencil, colored marker or crayon.

Optional: glitter, ribbon, and material.

What You Do:

1. Look through the magazines or cards for a picture that you like. You may find pictures of Santa Claus, or a child playing in the snow, or a beautifully wrapped present. When you find the right picture, cut it out.

2. Glue the picture onto your card.

Optional:

3. Draw in your own picture around the cut-out. For example, if you cut out a picture of a Christmas tree, you could draw a picture of a snowy forest, or your town, or your living room, around it.

4. Trim your card with glitter or small pieces of material or ribbon.

CHRISTMAS PHOTOGRAPHS

What You Need: a photograph of yourself (*and* permission to cut it up), scissors, glue, pencil, colored markers or crayons. (Note: You could have a picture taken especially for this card, and make as many copies of the photo as you need for the number of people you want to give it to. *It takes time to have film developed and reprints made.* Ask an adult for help.)

Optional: glitter, ribbon, material, magazine cut-outs.

What You Do:

1. Once you have the photograph, figure out how you want it shown on your card. You could:

Cut your whole self out of the photograph and place it on the front cover.

Or cut a small circle out of the front cover. Glue your photograph on the inside, so that your face shows through the hole in front.

Or cut out a picture from a magazine and stick your own picture on it. (This would make a very funny card.) For example, if you cut out a picture of a snowman, you could cut your head out of your photograph and put it where the snowman's head would be.

There are many creative ways to include your picture in a Christmas card.

2. Print your Christmas message in pencil, then go over it in colored marker or crayon.

Optional:

3. Trim your card with glitter, ribbon, or material.

How to Make
Christmas
Presents

Pin Cushion

This is an ideal gift for anyone who sews.

What you need: a styrofoam or sponge ball (about the size of a medium tomato), a piece of pretty cotton fabric that's large enough to fit easily over the ball, a long piece (about 12 inches [30 centimeters]) of yarn or ribbon, and scissors.

What You Do:

1. Place the styrofoam ball in the center of the fabric.

2. Bring the fabric up over the ball and gather all the ends together.

3. Tie the fabric ends tightly together with yarn or ribbon.

4. Snip the ends of the yarn or ribbon, if they're too long.

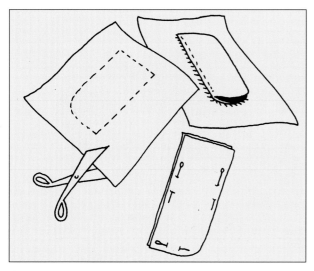

Trace the shape of the eyeglasses case on two pieces of felt. Cut around the outline and pin the two pieces together before sewing.

Felt Eyeglasses Case

If you know how to sew, this is a useful gift to make. For someone who wears glasses, an extra storage case is always handy.

What You Need: one borrowed eyeglasses case, two pieces of felt at least 7 inches long x 3½ inches (18 centimeters long x 9 centimeters wide), pen or pencil, needle, thread, scissors, and other small bits of material to sew on as decoration, and white glue.

What You Do:

1. Place the borrowed eyeglasses case on a piece of felt and trace around the edges with a pencil.

2. Repeat this step with a second piece of felt.

3. Carefully cut out the outlines on the two pieces of felt.

4. Match the two pieces, and pin together the edges of the two long and one of the short sides with straight pins.

5. While the felt is still pinned around the edges, test to see whether a pair of glasses will fit into your case. Slide them in gently. If the case is too small, start over. If it's too big, either trim the edges with scissors, or plan to sew your stitches further in from the edge.

6. With needle and thread, stitch up the two long sides and one short side of the case.

7. You can decorate the case by cutting small shapes from felt or other fabric, such as a flower or the initials of the person you're giving it to. Then simply glue them on. Let the glue dry.

8. If you borrowed someone else's glasses and glasses case, be sure to return them.

Tie your book together with pretty pieces of ribbon or wool.

A Book, By You!

If you like to write stories or poems, create your own book, which will become a treasured gift.

What You Need: scratch paper (for practicing your story), pen, nice white paper, construction paper, stapler or hole puncher, ribbon or yarn, scissors, glue.

Optional: (to illustrate your book): crayons or colored markers, pictures from magazines, or pieces of material.

What You Do:

1. Make up a short story, or write out a favorite tale you know. (There are good ones in this book.) Write your story on scratch paper first, as practice.

2. Write your story again on nice white paper. If you wish to illustrate your book, save room on the pages for your pictures.

Optional:

3. For a fancier look, write out your story on strips of nice white paper and glue each strip onto a larger piece of colored construction paper. If you wish to illustrate, save room on the construction paper for your picture.

Optional:

4. Here are three other ways to illustrate your story:

   a. with crayons or colored markers;

   b. with pictures cut out of magazines;

   c. with scraps of material or bright paper. (For example, you could make a house and yard with three pieces of material: a triangle set on top of a square or rectangle for the house, and a narrow strip of material with several cuts in it for the grass. Cut smaller rectangles for the doors and windows.)

It's also possible to mix your own drawing with scraps of material. For example, a piece of material in the shape of a triangle could become a girl's skirt, when glued to the drawing.

5. Make a book cover. Here are two ways:

   a. On a clean, separate piece of paper, print the title of your book, and your name, as author.

   b. On a large, clean piece of paper, create an illustration. Write the title and name of the author (you) on a smaller, separate strip of paper. Glue the strip onto the cover.

6. Gather together the cover and pages of your book. Bind them together in order on the left-hand side in either of the following ways:

   a. Staple the pages together at the top, middle, and bottom of the left edge. Glue a pretty strip of ribbon over the staples.

   b. Punch holes on each page at the top, middle, and bottom of the left edge, one sheet at a time. Try to have the holes in the same place on each page. Bind the pages together by threading bright yarn or ribbon through the holes and tying the ends in a knot.

The duckling wandered away from home, and found an old hut. It had a crooked door, and a thatched roof.

An old woman and her hen and cat lived there. The woman wanted the duckling to lay eggs for her to eat, for she was very poor and needed food.

Telephone Pad

What You Need: pad of paper, either 5 inches x 8 inches, or 4 inches x 6 inches (approximately 13 centimeters x 20 centimeters, or 10 centimeters x 15 centimeters); two pieces of cardboard or poster paper (both pieces the same size, and each a little bigger than the pad of paper); glue, and scissors. To decorate: your choice of colored markers, felt or other pieces of material, or poster paints.

What You Do:

1. Put your pad of paper on a larger piece of cardboard or poster paper. Cut out two pieces, one to cover the top of the pad and the other to cover the bottom.

2. Glue one piece of cardboard/poster paper to the bottom of the pad. Glue the other piece to the top of the pad, for the cover.

3. Decorate the cover with any of the materials suggested above.

Glue the pad of paper to a sturdy backing.

Decorate the top with a fanciful drawing.

© Christopher Bain 1988

Personalized Store-Bought Gifts

You can add a personal, homemade touch to many gifts that you buy in stores to make those presents extra special. Here are some suggestions:

Decorated Wastebaskets

What You Need: plastic or metal wastebasket, contact paper, glue, scissors. Optional: different colored pieces of felt, or other pretty pieces of material, ribbon.

What You Do:

1. Using the contact paper, cut out the design with which you wish to cover your wastebasket. Your design could be Christmas related, like a snowman or Christmas tree; or it could be a design that would be appropriate all year round, like flowers, boats, trains, or whatever you like best.

2. Peel the back of the contact paper off your cut-outs and stick each piece onto the wastebasket.

Optional:

3. Glue a pretty piece of ribbon around the top and bottom of the wastebasket.

4. If you do not use contact paper, you could make cutouts from other types of material like fabric. Apply glue to the back of each piece and stick it on the wastebasket. Make sure you let the glue dry.

Gifts With Painted Messages

On the outside bottom of a mug, bowl, plate, or cookie jar, there's room to paint a message like, "To Mom, Love from Your Favorite Christmas Elf, Eliza!"

What you need: newspapers, pencil, acrylic paint (not water-colors), thin-tipped paintbrush, and a cup of water.

What You Do:

1. Spread out the newspapers over your work space.

2. Lightly write your message in pencil on the bottom of your gift. If you make a mistake, you can erase it and try again. If pencil does not show up, practice writing your message on a piece of scratch paper to make sure it will fit on your gift.

3. Write the message on your gift in paint.

4. When finished painting, keep your gift turned upside down, so the paint can dry.

Painted Gardening Gloves

What You Need: a pair of plain, canvas gloves (available at most hardware stores), paper, pencil, newspaper, acrylic paint, and medium-sized paintbrush.

What You Do:

1. With a pencil and a piece of scratch paper, work out the design you wish to paint on your gloves. Try to keep your design simple, because there is not much room on the glove for detailed pictures. It will also be easier to paint.

2. Spread out newspaper over your work space.

3. With paintbrush and acrylic paints, paint your design on one glove, then the other. Because canvas is a rough surface, it may be necessary to go over your design more than once.

4. Let the gloves dry.

Painted Flowerpot

What You Need: a clay or plastic flowerpot (available at a hardware or discount store), poster or acrylic paint, newspaper, medium-sized paintbrush, paper, and pencil.

What You Do:

1. With a piece of paper and pencil, work out the design for your flowerpot. You can put a simple design or picture on one part of the pot, or you can carry the design all the way around.

2. Spread newspapers over your work space.

3. Paint the flowerpot, using your plan on paper to guide you.

4. Let the paint dry.

You can paint a cheerful picture or design on a flowerpot.

Photograph Key Chain

Your parents will love seeing a picture of you and your family on their key chain, every time they start the car or lock the front door.

What You Need: one key chain with a small, clear plastic or lucite frame attached (available at hardware or stationery stores), a picture that fits the key chain frame, scissors.

What You Do:

1. Find a few photographs that you think may fit the small clear frame. If the pictures do not belong to you, make sure that you have permission to take them and that no one wants the pictures back.

2. Take the pictures with you down to a hardware or stationery store, where a clerk will help you pick out a key chain.

3. You may have to cut off some of the photo to fit the frame—that's okay. And make sure the photo is secure in the key chain before giving it as a present.

Framed Picture

What You Need: a nice picture that you drew or an especially nice picture that you colored or painted from a book, and a picture frame (available at most discount stores).
Optional: construction paper or poster board.

What You Do:

1. Measure the size of the picture you wish to frame.

2. Take your picture, or just its measurements, with you when you go to the store to buy your frame. Pick the frame that will fit best.

3. If your picture is too big for the frame in the nearest size, you may need to trim the edges of your picture. If the picture is too small, choose a colorful piece of construction paper or poster board that fits neatly inside the frame. Tape your picture to that, then place the construction paper inside the frame.

© Christopher Bain 1988

Framed Photograph

This is for those with a camera. Many drugstores and photo stores can develop film in a day, sometimes less. If you wish to get the picture enlarged (made bigger), however, it may take more time.

What You Need: a nice photograph of either yourself or other family members (if the present is for someone in your family), and a picture frame to fit the picture (available at most discount stores).

What You Do:

1. Have someone take photos of you, or take a few pictures of the people you would like to put in your frame.

2. Get the film developed at any drugstore or photo store.

3. When the pictures come back, pick the one you like best. If you have the time and extra money, perhaps the picture would look good enlarged. The most common sizes for enlargements are 5 inches x 7 inches (13 centimeters x 17 centimeters), and 8 inches x 10 inches (20 centimeters x 25 centimeters). Ask the clerk at a camera store to show you the different sizes.

4. Buy the frame in the proper size for your picture. Discount stores have many types of frames, and the sizes are printed on the outside packaging.

HOW TO WRAP CHRISTMAS PRESENTS

Wrapping presents is a nice way of showing someone that you care about the present you are giving. It does not have to take a long time, and it should be fun. Have an adult help you the first time, until you get the knack.

Knowing how to cut the piece of paper to the right size and how to fold it around your gift will make wrapping much easier, and give you more time to decorate it later. Follow the instructions below to learn how to wrap a normal-sized present in a box. The next section will discuss different ways to wrap odd-shaped presents.

I. Wrapping Basics

What You Need: a roll or large sheet of wrapping paper, scissors, clear tape, a ruler.

What You Do:

1. After you've opened your wrapping paper, you may notice that there is a plain side (the "inside") and a colored or decorated side (the "outside").

2. Look at your box. There is a top, a bottom, and four sides. To cut a piece of wrapping paper the correct size, place your present so the *top* of the box is face-down on the inside of the wrapping paper 2–3 inches (5–8 centimeters) in from the edge of the paper.

3. Bring the rest of the paper over the present, until it meets up with the edge.

4. Make a crease in the paper where it meets the edge. Cut along the crease to the end of the paper.

You should now have a piece of paper that easily covers the top, bottom, and all sides of the box. The next steps will explain how to cut and fold the paper around the box.

5. Center your present on the piece of wrapping paper, with its top side down. There should be an equal amount of paper on the left and right sides of the box.

6. Check the ends of the paper to make sure there is enough to cover the ends of your box. To do that, take a ruler and measure how high the box is; then measure how much paper there is at either end. For example: If the box is one inch (2½ centimeters) high, there should be about 2 inches (5 centimeters) of paper at either end.

If one end is too short, simply move the box.

If one end is too long, take your scissors and trim the paper until it is the right size.

7. Now bring both sides of the paper up tightly, to the center of the top of the box. Put one side down over the other. Hold them together with one hand.

8. With the other hand, take a piece of tape and stick it on the box so that it holds both sides of the paper together. (Putting the tape on sideways will hold the paper together best.)

9. Add two or three more pieces of tape, so the paper on the box is held together securely.

10. With your thumbs, gently press one end of paper down against the edges of the box to crease it. This will make it easier to fold down the corners of the paper.

11. Take one corner and bring it up to the end side of the box. Press the corner fold down.

12. Do the same thing with the other corner. What you have now is a flap of paper at one end, which looks like an upside down triangle.

13. Bring the point of that triangle up the side to the top of the box and tape it down securely.

14. Now turn the box around and follow the same steps (11–14) for the other end.

Your present should now be wrapped and ready to decorate.

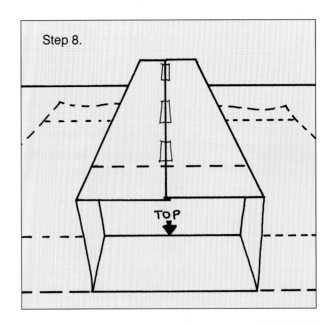

Step 8.

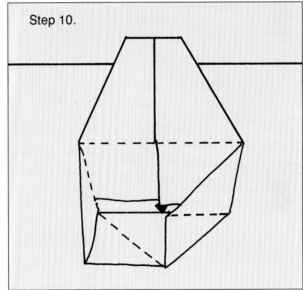

Step 10.

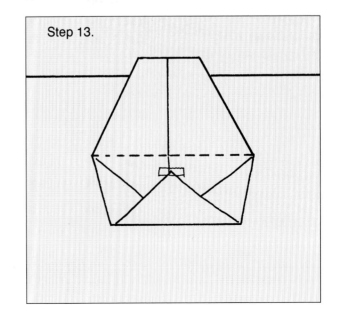

Step 13.

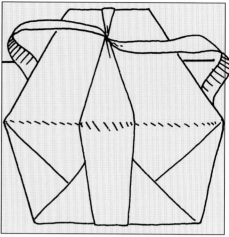

Tony Cenicola

II. How To Tie a Ribbon

Ribbons are a pretty way to complete the wrapping of a present. Ribbons come in many different materials, sizes, and colors, but the easiest way of tying them around a present is the same. Here's how you do it:

1. Take a long piece of ribbon. The ribbon should be long enough to be wrapped both lengthwise and widthwise around your present.

2. The top of your present should be facing up. With both hands holding onto the ribbon, slip it underneath the present. Bring the ribbon up and around the present, and even out the two ends until each of your hands is holding the same amount of ribbon.

3. Now, exchange ribbons: Take the ribbon in your right hand and give it to your left hand. Then take the ribbon in your left hand and give it to your right hand. When the ribbons are held up together, they should form an "X".

4. Bring the ribbons down and around your present making a cross on the top.

5. Turn the present upside down and tie the two ribbons together in a knot on the bottom. Snip the extra ribbon with scissors.

6. Take another piece of ribbon. This piece should be long enough to tie a bow, but give yourself a little extra ribbon, just in case.

7. Place your present right side up, and slip the new ribbon under the cross.

III. How To Wrap Odd-Shaped Presents

Some presents come in odd shapes and don't seem to fit into any available box. Here are some different ways to wrap those difficult gifts.

TISSUE PAPER GIFT WRAP

Tissue paper is very flexible, even when it's several layers thick. For that reason, it is easy to work with and good for wrapping odd-shaped presents.

What You Need: tissue paper, scissors, ribbon.

What You Do:

1. Roll your present up in tissue paper as best as you can. Make sure all the sharp angles are covered. Your present may look funny—that's okay.

2. Once all the sharp angles are covered up with the first wrapping, you may want to add a second layer of wrapping. This time, try wrapping as close as possible to the traditional method explained on page 64.

3. Tie a ribbon around your present.

4. Add a Christmas gift tag.

Tony Cenicola

COFFEE CAN, PAIL, OR FLOWERPOT GIFT WRAP

What You Need: an empty coffee can, pail, flowerpot, or similar container; tissue paper, ribbon, scissors, lightweight wrapping paper.

What You Do:

1. Put a layer or two of tissue paper inside your container, for decoration. It's okay if some of the paper sticks out of the container.

2. Crumple some more tissue paper and stick it in the bottom of the container. Crumpled paper will help cushion your present and prevent it from breaking.

3. Put your present inside the container. (You may wish to roll some tissue paper around your present before doing so.)

4. Fill the rest of the container up with tissue paper, until your present is completely covered.

5. Spread out a large sheet of wrapping paper, with the colored or patterned side facing down. The paper should be large enough to cover your container, plus a little extra; or, spread out several layers of fresh tissue paper over your work space.

6. Put your container in the middle of the paper with the top facing up.

7. Cut a long piece of ribbon and set it aside.

8. Bring all sides of the paper up over the center of the container.

9. Tie the paper sides together at the top with the ribbon.

10. Tie a bow with the ribbon, and add a Christmas gift tag.

Tony Cenicola

SHOPPING BAG GIFT WRAP

What You Need: one shopping bag, tissue paper, scissors, clear tape or stapler, ribbon.

What You Do:

1. Roll tissue paper around your present. (This is mostly for decoration.)

2. Lightly crumble some more tissue paper and put it at the bottom of your shopping bag. Keep adding tissue paper, until the bottom of the bag looks fluffy. Make sure there is enough paper to protect your present from breaking.

3. Place your present inside the bag.

4. Add some more slightly crumbled tissue paper on top of your present.

5. Seal the bag shut with tape, or with a stapler.

6. For decoration, add ribbons to the shopping bag handles. For more ideas on how to decorate your bag, see the suggestions on pages 70 and 71.

7. Add a Christmas gift tag.

PAPER CONE GIFT WRAP

This type of wrapping is best with small, lightweight presents.

What You Need: one piece of rectangular-shaped wrapping paper, clear tape, tissue paper.

What You Do:

1. Spread your wrapping paper out on your work space, with the inside of the paper facing upward.

2. Turn your paper so that the longer sides are on the top and bottom.

3. Using both hands, bring the bottom corners together toward the center and overlap one over the other. Do not fold the paper!

4. Pull the outside corner until the cone is the size you want.

5. Tape the outside corner to the cone.

6. Roll your present in tissue paper.

7. Stuff tissue paper or cotton into the bottom of the cone.

8. Place your present in the cone.

9. Cover your present with more tissue paper or cotton.

10. Add a Christmas gift tag.

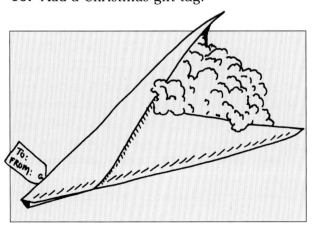

IV. How To Make Christmas Gift Tags

No present is complete until you include a small card or tag saying whom the gift is for and whom it is from. These tags are sold in stores along with gift wrapping and ribbons. It is also possible to make gift tags yourself. Here's how:

What You Need: a small scrap of wrapping paper, scissors and/or pinking shears, clear tape or thread.

What You Do:

1. Cut the scrap of wrapping paper into a square.

2. Fold the piece of paper in half with the undecorated or uncolored side on the inside. If necessary, trim the sides.

3. Your piece of paper should now open like a little book. On the inside, print the name of the person receiving the present, and then, of course, print your own name as the giver. For example, "To Grandma, Love, Michael."

4. To attach the tag, put a tiny hole at the top right hand corner. Slip a thread through the hole and tie it onto the ribbon wrapped around the present. OR: Tape the card to your present. Use either double-sided or regular, clear tape on the back.

Other Suggestions:

1. Make your tag a different shape: a circle, triangle, or even a Christmas tree. To do this, fold the wrapping paper in half, as explained earlier. Then cut out the shape you want—but be sure not to cut the fold. The fold holds the card together.

2. If your paper has an interesting design, fold your paper so the whole picture shows. Then cut around the picture—but remember not to cut the fold.

Tony Cenicola

V. Different Ways to Decorate Your Present

Tying a simple ribbon and bow on a present makes it pretty. But with a little extra time and thought, your present can have a personal touch, which makes the person receiving your gift feel special. Remember, though, not to spend *too* much time decorating your present, since your wrapping will probably not be saved. Just make decorating fun for yourself and the results will be good—and appreciated.

The following are ways to make your wrapping unique:

CHRISTMAS CUT-OUTS

What You Need: plain wrapping paper, patterned wrapping paper, ribbon, scissors, clear tape.

What You Do:

1. Find wrapping paper with a fun design on it for your cut-out. Large prints are usually easiest to work with.

2. Wrap your present in plain wrapping paper—but one that will go well with the patterned wrapping paper.

3. Tie a single ribbon, or two ribbons around your package. You may want to add a bow, but it's not necessary.

4. Cut out the design from the patterned wrapping paper. You can cut it out with plain scissors or pinking shears, for a zigzag edge.

Try all sorts of shapes, such as animals, houses, and people to make your wrapping paper unique. It's not always necessary to cut the design out perfectly; sometimes simply cutting *around* the design and including some of the background works just as well. You decide what would look best on your package, and how much time you want to spend cutting.

5. Place the cut-out on the package where you think it looks best, and tape it down. Perhaps one cut-out does not seem like enough. In that case, add more cut-outs. You can tape them anywhere on the package, or tape them all along the ribbon. Or, if you have tied a bow in the center, try placing cut-outs on either side of it.

PICTURES FROM MAGAZINES AND CHRISTMAS CARDS

What You Need: pictures from magazines and Christmas cards (get your parents' permission to cut them up), scissors, clear tape.

Optional: ribbon.

What You Do:

1. Go through the magazines or Christmas cards and look for a picture or photograph that you like. You might find some nice Christmas pictures, or a photograph that gives a little hint about what's inside your gift; or it might be just a funny illustration or cartoon that both you and the person receiveing your gift will enjoy.

2. Cut the picture out.

3. Figure out where to put the picture on your package. Stick the picture on with tape. (Using glue takes more time and can get messy.)

4. You could also frame the picture with ribbon. You can either tie the ribbon around your package to frame it, or cut and tape the ribbon to fit the edges of the picture.

CHRISTMAS TREE

What You Need: wrapping paper, scissors, clear tape.

Optional: light-colored construction paper and pen.

What You Do:

1. Choose a wrapping paper that will go well with the paper in which you wrapped your present.

2. Cut out a Christmas tree shape from the wrapping paper.

3. Tape it on your present.

Optional:

4. From light-colored construction paper, cut out a large star or Christmas tree ornament and tape it to the top of the Christmas tree.

5. Use the star or ornament as a Christmas present tag, which says whom the present is for and whom it is from.

CHRISTMAS TREE ORNAMENT

What To Do:

1. Make one of the Christmas tree ornaments in the section that starts on page 74.

2. Attach your ornament to your package. One way you can do this is by tying your ornament onto the ribbon around your gift. Loop thread or ribbon through the hole in your ornament and make a knot to hold it onto your package. Or use tape to stick your ornament on. (Tape works best with flat, lightweight ornaments.)

You can make Santa's face from easy paper shapes and a cotton puff.

SANTA CLAUS FACE

What You Need: plain or patterned wrapping paper, scissors, clear tape, cotton puff.

What You Do:

1. It's best to wrap your present in plain paper. Then, create the cut-outs for Santa's features in either patterned wrapping paper, or a different color of plain paper.

2. Cut out simple shapes to create Santa's features. For example: a large triangle for his cap, two small triangles for his eyes, a small square for his nose, a thin half-circle for his mouth, and another large triangle (turned upside down) for his beard. And two small circles for his rosy cheeks, and a cotton puff (or cut-out circle) for the top of Santa's cap.

3. Arrange Santa's face on your package.

4. Tape the different shapes onto the package.

VI. Invent Your Own Wrapping Paper

GLITTER PAPER

What You Need: old newspapers, wrapping paper, glue, glitter.

What You Do:

1. Wrap your present as you would normally, but do not add ribbon.

2. Spread out newspapers over your work space and put your present on top.

3. Lightly squeeze glue onto your present. (Make sure the glue does not dry before you apply the glitter.) You can write a message, draw a picture, or make a design with the glue. Or you can use words to make a pattern. For example, "Ho! Ho! Ho!" can be written all over the paper, in straight lines or at random.

You can also use glittery words in place of a Christmas tag, or draw a picture and write a message too.

4. Once you have applied the glue, quickly sprinkle the glitter over it. Put on more glitter than you need, so it covers every part of your picture or message.

5. Let the glue and glitter set for a minute or two. Then shake the glitter off onto the newspaper beneath your wrapping paper.

6. Let your design dry for another hour before touching it.

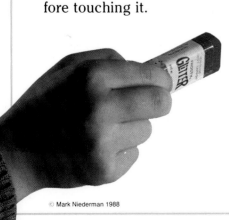

Painting your own wrapping paper with a pretty pattern will make your gift unique.

PAINTBRUSH PAPER

What You Need: newspaper, white drawing paper or newsprint, clear tape, poster paints or watercolors, a medium-sized or large-sized paintbrush, a small dish of water (to rinse off the brush).

What You Do:

1. Spread newspaper over your work space. Then bring out the rest of your materials.

2. Before you begin to paint, check to make sure the size of your drawing paper or newsprint paper will fit your present. If one sheet is too small, try taping two pieces together.

3. Paint simple designs on your paper. It's best to stick to designs, not pictures, so that the pattern will look right when you wrap your present. (A large picture might end up on the wrong side when you wrap your present.)

4. Let your painted paper dry before wrapping your present.

SPONGE PATTERN PAPER

What You Need: newspaper, regular-sized sponge or sponges, plain drawing paper or newsprint, poster paints, scissors, small dish of water.

Optional: glue and glitter.

What You Do:

1. Spread newspapers over your work space.

2. Check to see if one piece of drawing paper or newsprint is large enough to cover your present. If not, tape two (or more) pieces together.

3. Dampen a sponge and squeeze the extra water out.

4. With scissors, cut out a simple design—like a circle, triangle, or square.

5. Lightly dip one side of the sponge shape into a jar of poster paint.

6. Press the sponge's painted side down onto the paper. Press the sponge down again in another place to make a second print. Keep pressing the sponge down on the paper, making prints. You do not need to dip the sponge back into the paint each time — only when the print gets too light.

7. If you wish to change colors, rinse the sponge shape out in a small dish of water.

8. Let your paper dry completely before wrapping your present.

Other Suggestions:

a. Use different colors and different sponge shapes for more colorful paper.

b. Apply glue in and around your design and sprinkle glitter over it.

© Ann Hagen Griffiths 1987/Omni-Photo Communications

HOW TO MAKE CHRISTMAS TREE ORNAMENTS

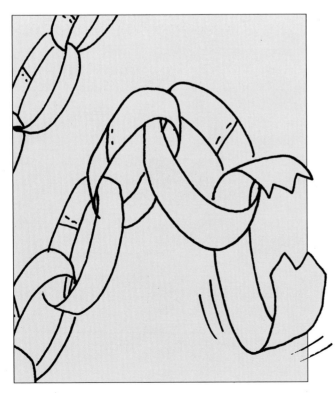

Insert a strip of paper through one link and tape it together. Keep adding links until your chain is as long as you desire.

Paper Chain

What You Need: colored construction paper or Christmas wrapping paper, and clear tape.

What You Do:

1. Cut the paper into equal-sized strips, about 1 inch wide and 8 inches long (2½ centimeters wide and 20 centimeters long).

2. Bring the ends of the strip together and hold them together in one hand.

3. Tape the ends together with your other hand.

4. Slip another strip through this ring and tape those ends together.

5. You can make the chain as long as you want by adding more strips.

Paper Cornucopia (Horn of Plenty)

What You Need: colored construction paper or sturdy Christmas wrapping paper, clear tape, glue, glitter, and a piece of thread.

What You Do:

1. Cut out a small rectangular piece of paper, about 5 inches wide and 4 inches long (13 centimeters wide and 10 centimeters long).

2. Decorate one side of the paper (if you're using Christmas paper, decorate the white side), with glitter. Concentrate your efforts on the upper left side of the paper, since that corner will be what shows most.

3. When dry, take the bottom two ends, *right corner over left corner,* and twist the paper until you have a little horn.

4. Punch a tiny hole at the top and insert a piece of thread.

5. Make a large loop with the thread and tie a knot.

6. Hang your paper cornucopia on the tree.

Felt Ornaments

What You Need: pencil, scissors, pins, squares of felt, sequins, glitter, glue, and thread.

What You Do:

1. On a piece of felt, draw the pattern outline of your ornament, such as a Christmas tree, angel, bell, star, or bulb.

2. Cut the felt around your pattern.

3. Now decorate the felt ornament as you wish. Sew or glue on sequins. Trim with glitter. Or make a face using other material or other colored pieces of felt.

4. Cut a tiny hole at the top and insert a piece of thread.

5. Make a loop with the thread and tie a knot.

6. Hang your felt ornament on the tree.

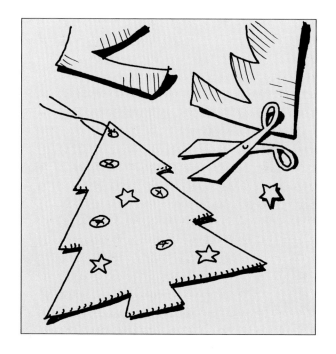

3. Now string your beads on the thread, stopping when there is only 1½ inches (4 centimeters) of thread left at the top.

4. Form the bead chain into a circle and tie the two ends together in a knot.

5. Cut the needle and any loose threads free, and your ornament is ready to hang on the tree.

Decorated Styrofoam Balls

What You Need: plain styrofoam balls, sequins, straight pins, ribbon, glitter, glue, scissors, and colored pipe cleaners.

What You Do:

1. Decorate the balls any way you like. You can attach sequins with straight pins, or glue on ribbons and glitter. You can make faces or pretty designs. Use your imagination!

2. When finished, cut a pipe cleaner in half (you may need an adult to help you). Stick it into the ball and bend the top, so it has a hook. Now it's ready to hang.

Bead Rings

What You Need: bright colored beads, needle, thread, and scissors.

What You Do:

1. Thread your needle with an approximately 6-inch-long (15-centimeter-long) piece of thread. (Make sure the needle fits through the holes in your beads.)

2. Bring the two ends together and tie a knot, about an inch (2½ centimeters) from the end.

Baby-in-a-Cradle Ornaments

What You Need: half a walnut shell, cotton puff, small pearl button, thin-tipped paint brush, acrylic or poster paint, glue, a small piece of material (about 1 inch or 2½ centimeters), string or slender ribbon, scissors, and clear tape.

What You Do:

1. Take half a walnut shell and put a cotton puff in it.

2. With a small paintbrush, paint two eyes and a small dot for a mouth on a small button.

3. When dry, glue the back of the button to the small piece of material, which will be a "blanket."

4. When dry, gently lift the blanket and button and place on top of the cotton puff.

5. Take a string or ribbon (about 10 inches [25 centimeters] long) and double it over. Tape the center of the ribbon to the bottom of the walnut.

6. Tie the string or ribbon in a large loop that extends well over the top of the walnut. Snip unnecessary ends, and hang your baby-in-a-cradle on the tree.

Tin Ornament

What You Need: a clean throwaway aluminum pan or a sheet of aluminum from the crafts store (tin foil is too soft); thick felt markers; shellac or clear nail polish; yarn.

What You Do:

1. First draw your pattern on the aluminum sheet.

2. Cover your work space with newspaper, and place the aluminum sheet on top.

3. Cut out the design on the aluminum.

4. Color it with markers.

5. To finish, use shellac or clear nail polish to coat the surface.

6. Make a small hole at top (with pen point or the tip of a knitting needle).

7. Loop bright yarn or thread through hole and secure with knot. Now it's ready to hang.

Use colored markers to decorate a shiny tin ornament.

Christmas Tree Bulbs

What You Need: clear glass Christmas tree bulbs (ball-shaped glass ornaments); your favorite small Christmas accessories or toys; and ribbons, cotton, sequins, glitter, and glue.

What You Do:

1. Remove the top (hook part) from the bulb.

2. Fill the bulb with such things as: cotton puffs, a sprig of holly or mistletoe, a small toy, or bright strands of ribbon. You can also add a small picture. Simply roll it up and stick it through the top—it will unfold inside.

3. If you wish, decorate the outside of the bulb—though be sure not to cover up what you put inside. Lightly coat part of the bulb with glue, then sprinkle on some glitter. Or glue a ribbon around the center. Let the bulb dry.

4. When finished, put the top back on. Then hang on the tree.

Note: It's also nice to put a personal touch on other types of ornaments. There's often room for painting a message, such as your name or "Merry Christmas," and the year.

If the ornament is a gift, paint the name of the person to whom you are giving it, and any other message you wish.

HOW TO MAKE CHRISTMAS DECORATIONS FOR YOUR HOME

A Christmas tree in the living room and yummy aromas coming from the kitchen help set the holiday mood in any home. But you can create even more seasonal spirit by adding decorative touches of your own. The following pages show a variety of fun ways to do this.

GLUING TIPS

White Glue that comes in a plastic, squeeze-type bottle is good for almost every project listed in this book. It is easy to handle and sticks well to most objects.

White glue is good for working with glitter. You can use the tip of the bottle like a pen or pencil, to write or draw with the glue. Then simply sprinkle on the glitter.

Rubber Cement is better to use than white glue when working with paper. White glue sticks fast and hard when two pieces of paper are glued together. For that reason, the paper is hard to pull apart, if you have made a mistake, and you will almost always have to start over again. Also, if white glue comes out around the edges, it will leave a mark; rubber cement can be gently rubbed off when dry and will not leave a mark.

Rubber cement is also good for gluing other things onto paper. If you make a mistake, it's possible to gently pull the item off the paper, gently rub the rubber cement off both pieces, and start over again—your mistake will hardly show.

Rubber cement also sticks better than regular white glue, when gluing two pieces of felt together.

Rubber cement, which usually comes with a brush attached to the bottle cap, is easy to apply to large surfaces. However, the big brush makes it hard to apply to small items, such as narrow ribbons and sequins. The brush also makes rubber cement less effective than white glue when working with those items that you sprinkle with glitter.

When working with either type of glue, remember not to apply too much of it. Too much glue makes a decoration look sloppy, especially when it comes out around the edges. You can always add more glue later.

Christmas Table Centerpieces—A festive touch to a holiday table.

What You Need: sturdy paper, scissors, pencil, straight pins, felt.
Optional: sequins, yarn, ribbon, different colored felt, and white glue.

What You Do:

1. On a large piece of paper (8 inches x 10 inches [20 centimeters x 25 centimeters]), draw a simple object or figure, such as a Christmas tree, star, angel, or poinsettia.

2. Cut the drawing out and place it on a large piece of felt.

3. Pin the drawing to the felt and cut around the pattern.

4. Decorate the felt Christmas shape as you like. You can glue on sequins, trim the edges with yarn or ribbon, and add smaller cut-out shapes of felt.

Christmas Stockings

Your own personally decorated stocking to hang up on the fireplace.

(Note: This makes a fine decoration, but it may not be sturdy enough for Santa to fill.)

What You Need: a piece of red felt twice as big as your stocking will be, heavy paper, straight pins, pencil, yarn, other pieces of different colored felt or fabric, and white glue.

What You Do:

1. Draw a pattern for the stocking on a heavy piece of paper.

2. Cut the pattern out.

3. Fold the red felt in half (or place two equal-sized pieces together).

4. Pin the paper stocking pattern to the felt.

5. Cut carefully around the pattern. When you finish, you should have two stocking-shaped pieces of felt.

6. Decorate the felt stocking pieces. Make sure you only decorate the outside portion of each piece. With the other colored pieces of felt or fabric, you can cut out letters to make your name, or simple Christmas objects like a star, ornament, Christmas tree or present. If you know how to sew, use a needle and thread to attach sequins. Trim with colorful yarn, which you can glue on.

7. After decorating the outer side of each stocking piece, glue the two sides together. Put the glue along only the outside edge of the undecorated side of one of the stockings. Make sure not to glue the top edges together. Press the two pieces together. For extra strength, sew the two sides together carefully.

8. To hang, snip a small hole in the upper right hand corner of each side of the stocking. Pull a piece of yarn through, and tie it in a loop.

"Klockastrang" or "Bell Pull"

A festive door decoration that announces visitors' arrival with the jingle of bells when the door is opened.

This decoration can be as large as you like, but beginners may want to start with something small. A good size would be 10 inches wide x 12 inches long (25 centimeters wide x 30 centimeters long).

What You Need: a piece of green, white, or red felt, measuring 10 inches x 12 inches (25 centimeters x 30 centimeters), scissors, straight pins, yarn, smaller pieces of colored felt or other fabric, ribbon, glue, small "jingle bells," needle and thread.

What You Do:

1. Decorate the Klockastrang in the same ways suggested for the Christmas stocking. You may also want to glue ribbon strands down the front. Sew the jingle bells along the edges.

2. To make a handle, cut a small hole out in the top center. Pull a piece of yarn through and tie it in a loop.

Hang a klockastrang on the door to hear a jingle each time it opens or closes.

Christmas Place Cards

What You Need: last year's Christmas cards, table place cards, and glue or clear tape.

What You Do:

1. Cut out an object (an ornament, Christmas tree, candy cane) or a figure (Baby Jesus, Santa Claus, or animal) from the old Christmas cards.

2. Put glue or tape onto the back of the cut-out, where it will stick to the place card.

3. Stick the cut-out onto the place card.

© Mark Niederman 1988

Snowball Tree

What You Need: styrofoam cone (available in crafts stores), green construction paper, cotton balls, toothpicks or straight pins, glue (and possibly, clear tape), and glitter.

What You Do:

1. Take a styrofoam cone and wrap it in the construction paper. To do this, fold the paper around the cone, tucking the upper right hand corner of the paper around the point of the cone. Bring the rest of the paper around the cone and tape the two sides together.

If your paper does not completely cover the cone, patch the space with a small square of green construction paper. Stick the patch over the space with tape or glue.

2. Stick the cotton balls onto the cone with straight pins or toothpicks.

3. Lightly dab some glue onto the edge of the cotton balls.

4. Sprinkle glitter over the glue.

5. Let your "tree" dry completely before moving it.

Place your picture right-side-up on the sticky side of the clear contact paper.

Then place the sticky side of the second *piece of contact paper down on top of the picture.*

Holiday Table Mat

This table mat (or place mat) wipes off easily and can be used over and over. Make the mat any size you like. Take a ruler and measure a table mat at home. The size suggested in these directions, 17 inches wide x 11½ inches high (43 centimeters wide x 29 centimeters high), will allow some of the picture to show, even when covered with a plate.

The clear contact paper called for is available at most hardware stores.

What You Need: a piece of drawing paper in the size suggested above, clear contact paper (enough to cover *both* sides of your paper), a ruler, crayons or markers, construction paper, sequins, glitter, and glue.

What You Do:

1. On the paper, draw a picture with Christmas as the theme. You could also use colored construction paper to cut out and paste on small objects, such as Christmas trees and Snowflakes.

2. Glue on some sequins and glitter, if you like.

3. With a ruler, measure the size of your picture. Let's say your picture is the suggested size, 17 inches wide x 11½ inches high (43 centimeters high x 29 centimeters wide).

4. Spread out your contact paper. With your ruler, measure and cut out a piece 17½ inches wide x 12 inches high (44 centimeters wide x 30 centimeters high). (It's good to have a little extra around the edges.)

5. Measure and cut out another piece of contact paper, the same size as the first.

6. Before applying the contact paper, make sure your picture is clean and that any paint or glue has dried. Peel the contact paper off its backing sheet and lay it on your work space so the sticky side is facing up.

7. You may want to ask an adult to help you place the back side of your picture on top of the contact paper, as straight and evenly as possible.

8. Peel backing off your second piece of contact paper. Lay the contact paper on your work space, sticky side up.

9. Place the front of your picture down on the sticky side of the second contact sheet. Try to match the sides and corners as well as possible.

10. Trim any edges of the contact paper that don't match.

© Mark Niederman 1988

Many beautiful designs can be created by making cuts in a piece of folded paper.

Snowflakes

What You Need: paper (plain or colored), scissors.

Optional: pretty thread or yarn.

What You Do:

1. Cut a circle from a piece of paper.

2. Fold it in half.

3. Fold it in half again.

4. Cut out shapes along the folds.

Optional:

1. For a Christmas tree ornament, punch a small hole at the top and put a piece of thread or yarn through it. Tie the string to make a loop and hang your snowflake on the tree.

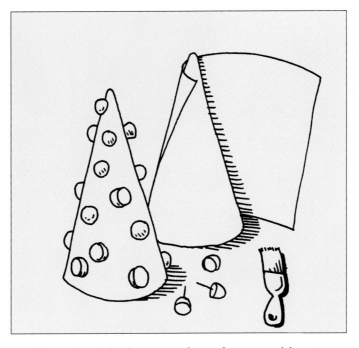

*Wrap a piece of colored paper around a styrofoam cone and decorate
it with gum drops.*

Sugarplum Tree

What You Need: a styrofoam cone, scissors, clear tape or glue, colored construction paper, paste, glitter, toothpicks, gumdrops, marshmallows.

What You Do:

1. Wrap the styrofoam cone in the paper. To do this, fold the paper around the cone, tucking the upper right corner around the point of the cone.

2. Bring the rest of the paper around the cone and tape the two sides together. If your paper does not completely cover the cone, patch the space with a small square of green construction paper. Stick the patch over the space with tape or glue.

3. Lightly brush on paste.

4. Sprinkle glitter over the cone.

5. Place a gumdrop and a small marshmallow on a toothpick and stick it onto the cone. Keep adding these until the cone tree is full.

Pomander Ball

A nice and easy decoration that also adds the scent of Christmas to your house. Try hanging it in your closet or bathroom, or the entrance to your house.

What You Need: an apple or orange, box of whole cloves, small bag, 1 tablespoon cinnamon, 1 tablespoon orris root (available at most pharmacies), and yarn or ribbon.

Optional: tissue paper.

What You Do:

1. Take a whole, unpeeled apple or orange and stick the cloves into the fruit. (The cloves absorb the fruit juices, so the fruit won't rot.)

2. Keep sticking in cloves, until the whole fruit is covered.

3. Fill a small bag with 1 tablespoon of cinnamon and 1 tablespoon of powdered orris root and shake the clove-covered fruit in it.

© Mark Niederman 1988

Optional:

4. Wrap your pomander ball in pretty tissue paper.

5. Tie a pretty ribbon or bright yarn around the ball.

Picture Pencil Holder

What You Need: an empty, clean orange juice concentrate can, construction paper or plain-colored wrapping paper or contact paper, clear tape, scissors, paper doily, yarn, glue, and a small close-up photograph or drawing of yourself.

What You Do:

1. Wrap the can in construction paper, wrapping paper, or contact paper. To do this, hold one end of a piece of your paper next to the can and wrap the other end around it.

2. Tape the two sides of paper together (not necessary for contact paper). If there is extra paper up top, simply push it down inside the can. Smooth the extra paper until it lies flat against the can.

3. Cut the picture of yourself into an oval shape.

4. Cut the paper doily into an oval shape, slightly bigger than your picture.

5. Paste your picture onto the oval doily. Let it dry.

6. Paste the doily/picture onto the can.

7. Add colorful yarn or string around the top and bottom.

Pretty Things to Do with Tree Branches and Pine Cones

These ideas are simple yet lovely ways to make use of leftover Christmas tree branches, as well as bare branches and pine cones that have fallen off trees.

GOLD BRANCHES

What You Need: evergreen branch, clean sponge, newspaper, paintbrush, gold paint, and a vase.

What You Do:

1. Spread out newspaper over your work space.

2. Take an evergreen branch and cut off its lower leaves or needles.

3. Wipe the other needles clean with a damp sponge and let them dry.

4. Paint the whole branch, or just the tips—whichever you like.

5. Fill a vase with water, and put the bare ends in it.

GUMDROP BRANCHES

What You Need: prickly, thorny branches; gumdrops; and a vase.

What You Do:

1. Wash and dry the branches. Be careful not to prick yourself.

2. Stick a small gumdrop on each thorn.

3. Put in a vase with *no* water.

GLITTER BRANCHES

For these branches, you can use either regular white glue or a paste made from flour and water that you put on with a paintbrush.

The flour-and-water paste creates a kind of "snow" effect and also glues on the glitter. Though it doesn't go on as smoothly as white glue, it's white color will last.

To make the paste, mix 1 tablespoon flour and 2 teaspoons water in a small dish or cup.

White glue goes on smoothly and holds the glitter well. However, its white color soon disappears and will no longer look like snow.

What You Need: a bare branch with small twigs on it, a small paintbrush, newspaper, flour-and-water paste (described above).

What You Do:

1. Spread out newspaper over your work space.

2. Paint part of the branch with the flour-and-water paste (or white glue).

3. Shake glitter over the branch.

4. Let the branches dry.

5. Put in a vase with *no* water.

DECORATED PINE CONES

What You Need: newspaper, glue (or the flour-and-water paste described in Glitter Branches), pine cones, white paint, paintbrush, sequins, tweezers, glitter, and silver or gold string.

What You Do:

1. Spread newspaper over your work space.

2. To give the appearance of "snow," paint the pine cone edges white. Let the paint dry.

3. Weave gold or silver thread around the pine cone petals, from top to bottom.

4. Squeeze glue over the pine cone petals—do not let dry.

5. Sprinkle glitter over the glue.

6. Glue on sequins. For placing sequins in difficult places, use a pair of tweezers.

Letter to Santa Claus

What You Need: a piece of construction paper, paste or glue, glitter, and stick-on stars in various colors.

What You Do:

1. On a piece of paper, write a message to Santa in glue. Use a brush for paste or squeeze out the glue from a squirt-type container. Do not let the adhesive dry. If you have a long message, write one line, go on to step 2, then write the next line.

2. Sprinkle the message with glitter. Make sure the glitter is a different color from your paper. For best results, use a dark-colored glitter on light-colored paper.

3. Add a few stick-on stars, placing them as you like.

HOLIDAY CRAFTS AND RECIPES 88

The Drummer Boy's Drum

What You Need: an empty oatmeal box; wrapping paper, construction paper, or contact paper; yarn; clear tape; glue; and scissors.

What You Do:

1. Remove the lid from the box.

2. Cut a piece of wrapping paper, construction paper, or contact paper large enough to fit around your box.

3. Hold one side of the paper against the box, and bring the other side of the paper around. Tape the two sides together.

4. If your paper goes over the top of the box, simply push the paper down and flatten it against the inside of the box.

5. Place the unwrapped lid on the box. (The drum sounds better with an unwrapped lid.)

Optional:

6. Decorate the drum by gluing on yarn or ribbon.

Balloon Ball

All your friends will want to know how you made this interesting decoration.

What You Need: a balloon (not *too* big, until you know how to make them); several yards of thick green, red, and white string; a dish of glue or liquid starch; a large bowl; cotton puffs; sprig of mistletoe or holly, or a lightweight Christmas ornament.

What You Do:

1. Blow up a small balloon and tie the end in a knot.

2. Dip the strings, one at a time, in the glue or liquid starch and coil the wet strings around the balloon so that the whole balloon is covered.

3. Set the stringy, wet balloon in a large bowl and let it dry. This may take several days.

4. When the strings are dry, pop the balloon.

5. Carefully remove the balloon pieces. What's left is a coiled string ornament.

6. You can tie a string through it and hang it from your ceiling.

7. Before hanging, cut a small hole in the bottom.

8. Put a fluffy layer of cotton inside and add a sprig of mistletoe, holly, or a lightweight Christmas ornament.

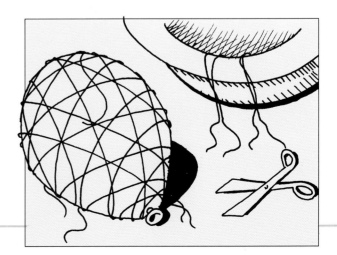

Christmas Countdown Chain

What You Need: scissors, construction paper or wrapping paper.

What You Do:

1. Make a holiday paper chain (see directions on page 74), 25 links long, and number each link from 1 to 25.

2. Beginning December 1, take off one link each day, starting with the link numbered 25. (Or make the chain 50 links long and take off two links every day.)

3. Watch the chain grow shorter and shorter, as Christmas Day grows closer and closer.

Macaroni Wreath

What You Need: a paper plate; watercolors, poster paints, or gold paint; a paintbrush; a box of macaroni; glue; scissors; newspaper; ribbon.

What You Do:

1. Cut a circle from the center of the paper plate.

2. Glue the raw macaroni around the plate. Let the glue dry.

3. Paint the macaroni with watercolors, poster paints, or gold paint. Let the paint dry.

4. Loop a ribbon through the center of the wreath and tie it in a bow.

HOW TO MAKE AN ADVENT CALENDAR

Advent calendars are a German custom that has been carried over to North America and England. An Advent calendar is a special way of marking the days from December 1 until Christmas Eve or Christmas Day.

Most Advent calendars are large Christmas pictures with twenty-four or twenty-five little windows cut into them. Before December 1, all the windows are closed, so that the outside of each one blends into the picture. But starting December 1, a window is opened each day until Christmas.

Each window is numbered, so that you know which window to open on what day. (For example, on December 5, you open Window 5.) Behind each window is a different picture, and it's always a surprise to see what the picture is.

Here's how to make your own:

What You Need: drawing paper, pencils, crayons or colored markers, scissors, clear tape or glue, and glitter.

What You Do:

1. Using a pencil, draw a Christmas scene on a large piece of paper. The scene can be anything you like—your home or town, an imaginary Christmas tree forest with fairies and elves, Santa Claus up at his North Pole workshop, or the Nativity scene, with Mary, Joseph, the shepherds, and three wise men looking at the Baby Jesus in the manger.

Instead of a Christmas scene, you can also draw a large figure like a Santa Claus, a Christmas tree, or even a giant gingerbread boy.

2. Once you have a picture you like, lightly pencil in twenty-four or twenty-five little windows. The windows can be any size that best fits your page. Remember, though, that if you make a tiny window, the picture behind it will have to be tiny also.

To make a medium-sized window, draw three sides of a box: a 1-inch (2½-centimeter) line going sideways, a ¾-inch (2-centimeter) line going lengthwise, and another 1-inch (2½-centimeter) line going sideways.

Make the ¾-inch (2-centimeter) line on the right-hand side, so the window will open from right to left.

3. Number the windows.

4. Go over your drawing in crayon or colored marker. (Be careful not to lose your window lines.)

5. Cut the three sides to your windows. This part can be tricky; do it slowly, or ask an adult to help you, so you do not tear your drawing. Once that part is done, the outside of your Advent calendar is complete.

6. For the little pictures behind the windows, take out one or two clean sheets of drawing paper. Use this paper to make twenty-four or twenty-five drawings that will fit behind the squares on your Christmas picture. Make the space between each drawing at least as big as the window box.

The drawings can be related to your picture or simply drawings of Christmas or the whole holiday season. Other suggestions might include a picture (or the name) of a friend, grandparent, pet, or anyone special in your life.

7. Cut around each picture with enough extra space to cover the back of the window.

8. Tape or lightly glue the border of each drawing to the back side of the calendar, over a window square. The picture should be facing down; that way, when the window is opened from the front, the picture will show there.

9. Your Advent calendar is finished! But if you wish, trim your picture and the windows with a little glitter.

How to Cook Christmas Treats

Before You Start to Cook

- Ask an adult if it is all right to use the kitchen.
- Be sure to wash your hands.
- Read the recipe carefully to make sure you understand it.
- Check the list of ingredients your recipe calls for—do you have them all?
- Check to see if you have all the cooking tools (cutting board, the right size pan, etc.) your recipe calls for.
- Put on an apron to keep your clothes clean.

While You Are Cooking

- Ask an adult before you use a sharp knife, can opener, electric mixer, stove, or oven.
- Use pot holders to protect your hands when handling any dish that has been on the stove or in the oven.
- When cooking on the stove, keep the handles of pots and pans turned toward the side of the range to avoid knocking into them and causing spills.

- Use a cutting board when slicing or chopping ingredients. Do not cut anything on the counter, unless you have permission from an adult to do so.
- Be sure to ask for help, when . . .
    —you need to pour batter from a large, heavy bowl into a pan;
    —you need to pour liquid from a large, heavy bottle or carton;
    —you are unsure about a certain measurement or ingredient.

When You Finish Cooking

Try to make the kitchen look as clean as, (or cleaner than!) when you began. To do this:

- Wash all the dishes, pans, and tools you used.
- Take a sponge and wipe the counter top clean. You may also need to wipe around the stove and on the oven and refrigerator doors.
- Put away all remaining ingredients.

John Pemberton

© Christopher Bain 1988

Cooking Tools You May Need

FOR PREPARATION:

Knife
Cutting board
Wooden spoon
Rubber spatula or scraper
Metal or non-stick spatula
Bowls: large, medium, and small
Saucepans: medium and small
Blender
Electric mixer
Rolling pin

FOR MEASURING:

Measuring spoons (¼, ½, 1 teaspoon; 1 tablespoon)
Measuring cups for dry ingredients (¼, ⅓, ½,
1 cup)
Measuring cups for liquid ingredients

FOR BAKING:

Bread loaf pan
13-inch x 9-inch rectangular pan
8-inch square pan
8-inch round cake pan
13-inch x 9-inch baking sheet

Measuring Hints

- Use measuring cups for liquids when a recipe calls for ¼ cup or more of milk, water, juice, or vegetable oil. Put the cup down on a counter or table and pour the liquid until it reaches the proper mark on the measuring cup. Look at the mark at eye level to make sure it is right.

- Use measuring cups for dry ingredients such as sugar (white, brown, and confectioners), flour, and any other type of dry substance, when the recipe calls for ¼ cup or more. When the recipe calls for less than ¼ cup of something, use measuring spoons.

- When measuring salt, pour gently from the box while standing over the sink or waste basket. If you don't have a box of salt, shake a good amount of salt from a salt shaker into a cup and dip your measuring spoon into that. When a recipe calls for ⅛ teaspoon salt, measure it with the spoon marked "⅛ teaspoon," or fill the spoon marked "¼ teaspoon" halfway.

- When measuring baking soda, baking powder, cornstarch, or spices, dip the measuring spoon into the can. Then level the top off with a butter knife.

- When measuring butter, read the markings on the wrapping of a new stick of butter or margarine. Or, leave the butter out of the refrigerator until it is soft enough to be scooped into a measuring cup or spoon.

- When doubling or halving a recipe:

    If you want to make twice as much food as a recipe in this book will make, you will have to double the amount of each ingredient. For example, if the recipe calls for one egg, use two. If it calls for 1½ teaspoons salt, use 3.

    When you want to make only half as much food as a recipe will make, use half the amount of each ingredient the recipe calls for. For example, if it calls for 1 teaspoon, use only ½ teaspoon. If it calls for 4 cups, use 2.

If a recipe calls for 1 egg, and you need to divide it in half, crack the egg in a separate bowl, and beat it with a fork. When the yolk and white are mixed well, you can pour half into your recipe.

The measurements provided below should help you with your kitchen arithmetic.

Measuring Equivalents

3 teaspoons = 1 tablespoon
4 tablespoons = ¼ cup or 2 fluid ounces
8 tablespoons = ½ cup or 4 fluid ounces
8 ounces = 1 cup
16 ounces = 2 cups
2 cups = 1 pint
2 pints (4 cups) = 1 quart
4 quarts = 1 gallon

© Christopher Bain 1988

The picture above shows (from top to bottom) one level teaspoon and two heaping teaspoons which are described on page 99. It's easy to see that a heaping teaspoon is a very imprecise measure.

© Mark Niederman 1988

John Pemberton

A Kid's Glossary of Cooking Tips, Terms, and Ingredients

Bake—to cook in an oven.

Beat—to mix rapidly, stirring many times with a spoon or an electric beater.

Blend—to combine two or more ingredients thoroughly.

Brown Sugar—There are two main types of brown sugar, light and dark. These sugars are moister than white or "granulated" sugar. They also have a stronger flavor, especially dark brown sugar.

Brown sugar is lumpy and must be measured in a certain way. To do it right, spoon the sugar into a measuring cup and press down on it with your hand to pack it in. When the sugar is level with the top of the cup, the measurement is correct.

Make sure to store brown sugar in a tightly closed plastic bag in the refrigerator, for it tends to dry out and harden easily.

Butter—Real butter is a product made from milk or sweet cream. Margarine, which is similar to butter, is made mostly from vegetable oils. In this book, when a recipe calls for "butter," you can substitute margarine instead.

Chop—to cut into little pieces with a knife, blender, or food processor. Make sure you have an adult's permission before you chop.

Confectioners Sugar—also called **pow-dered** or **icing sugar.** This sugar resembles flour and is most often used in making frostings. If you don't have any, buy some! Regular white or brown sugar won't work as a substitute.

Flour—Some recipes will call for you to **grease and flour a baking pan.** To do this, spread the pan with butter or shortening (see "Grease" below), and drop about a tablespoon of flour into the pan. Holding the pan over the sink, shake it until the flour is spread evenly around the pan. It helps to hold the pan in one hand and use the other to tap the pan.

To flour a rolling pin, take a little butter or vegetable oil and rub it on the rolling pin. Then sprinkle a little flour on the pin with your hand. The flour should prevent your dough from sticking to the pin.

Granulated sugar or **white sugar**—This is the most common type of sugar. It is smooth, like sand, and pours easily into measuring cups without having to be firmly packed down by hand.

Grease—Some recipes will call for you to **grease a baking pan**: take a slice of butter and use a piece of paper towel to spread it evenly over the sides and bottom of the pan. Greasing helps prevent your baked goods from sticking to the pan.

Melt—heat a substance (like butter) in a pot or pan until it becomes liquid.

Non-stick pans—These kinds of pans, available at most hardware or discount stores, usually do not need to be floured or greased to prevent sticking. But it's not a bad idea to lightly grease your pan, anyway.

Separating An Egg — Sometimes a recipe calls for just an egg yolk or just an egg white. It is then necessary to separate the two different parts. To do this:

1. Take out two small bowls.

2. Gently crack the eggshell on the side of one bowl as evenly as possible, so that you get two equal halves. One half of the egg shell should contain all egg white. The other half should contain the egg yolk, plus some more egg white.

3. Let the egg white from the first half drip into one of the bowls. Keep the other half of the eggshell upright. It is important not to let any yolk mix in with the white.

4. When the eggshell with the egg white is empty, transfer the egg yolk to that shell half. In doing so, try to let some of the extra egg white from the second shell drip into the egg white bowl.

5. Keep shifting the egg yolk from one eggshell half to the other, until all the extra egg white is in the first bowl. Then very gently slip the egg yolk from the shell and into the second bowl.

Sift—This usually refers to putting flour through a sifter, or sieve, which makes the flour smoother. It is possible to buy pre-sifted flour; it will say "pre-sifted" on the package. If you don't have a sifter, stir the flour with a fork to get out any lumps.

Spoonfuls (Level, Heaping, and Rounded)—Some of the following recipes call for these types of measurements:

Level—To measure a level teaspoonful (or half-teaspoonful or tablespoonful) of a recipe ingredient, scoop up some of the ingredient in the appropriate measuring spoon, and level it off (make it even with the top edges of the spoon) with a butter knife or another spoon. All recipes call for level spoonfuls unless they say otherwise.

Heaping—This means the measurement does not have to be precise. Scoop up the ingredient in the appropriate teaspoon or tablespoon, but DON'T level it off.

Rounded—Cookies are often dropped by "rounded teaspoonfuls" onto a baking sheet. To do this, dip a teaspoon into the dough. Then, using your fingers or another spoon, push the cookie dough from the teaspoon onto the baking sheet. Place each small ball of dough about an inch or more away from the last one, if the recipe calls for it. Cookie dough spreads out as it bakes; placing the dough balls far apart will prevent them from spreading out to become one big cookie!

© Lynn Karlin 1987

HOLIDAY CRAFTS AND RECIPES 100

Christmas Party Cones

1 regular-sized box any flavor cake mix
Any ingredients the cake mix calls for
24 flat-bottomed ice cream cones
Frosting (any flavor)

1. Heat oven to 350 degrees F., and have ready baking sheets or muffin tins large enough to hold 24 ice cream cones.

2. Prepare the cake mix in a medium bowl. Follow the directions on the box, but do not pour the batter into a pan or bake it.

3. Fill the ice cream cones with cake batter. To do this, hold each ice cream cone in one hand over the bowl. Spoon cake batter into the cone until it is half full. Place the filled cones on baking sheets or in the cups of muffin tins.

4. Bake for 30 minutes. Let cool before frosting. (For frosting recipes, see page 103.)

Makes 24 cones.

Easy Egg Nog

This traditional Christmas drink tastes a lot like a vanilla milkshake.

4 cups milk
4 eggs
2 teaspoons vanilla extract
3 tablespoons sugar
2 cups vanilla ice cream
Nutmeg

1. Pour all the ingredients into a blender.

2. Cover and blend for 1 minute.

3. Pour into 4 glasses and sprinkle the top of each glass with nutmeg.

Rich Hot Chocolate

This recipe for this wintertime favorite may take longer to make than "instant" hot chocolate, but it tastes richer and more choco-latey.

3 tablespoons unsweetened cocoa powder
3 tablespoons sugar
⅛ teaspoon salt
½ cup water
3½ cups milk
Marshmallows

1. In a medium-sized saucepan mix together the cocoa, sugar, and salt.

2. Add the water and stir over low heat, until lumps disappear.

3. Add the milk, and heat the mixture over low heat. When tiny bubbles appear around the edge of the pan, turn off the heat. Do not let the milk boil.

4. Make some foam by taking a whisk and briskly whipping the hot chocolate in the pan.

5. The marshmallows may be added before or after pouring the hot chocolate into the mugs.

Makes 4 servings.

Candy Cane Frosting

1 pound confectioners (powdered) sugar
½ cup softened or melted butter
2 tablespoons milk
1½ teaspoons peppermint extract
4 medium-sized candy canes OR 15 small, round, hard, red-
   and-white peppermint candies

1. In a large bowl, with an electric mixer, mix together all ingredients until smooth. Put bowl aside for a moment.

2. Ask an adult to help you with this part. In a small paper or plastic bag, crush the candy with a hammer. Be careful not to pound on the candy too hard or the bag may rip.

3. Set aside some of the crushed candy bits for the topping. Add most of the bits to the frosting and stir with a wooden spoon. Sprinkle the remaining bits on top of the cake, cupcakes, or muffins.

Makes enough frosting for 1 cake or 24 muffins or cupcakes.

Chocolate Butter Frosting

3 tablespoons butter
2 tablespoons unsweetened powdered cocoa
¼ cup hot water
⅛ teaspoon salt
1 cup confectioners (powdered) sugar
1 teaspoon vanilla extract

1. Melt the butter in a medium saucepan on the stove, over low heat.

2. Add and blend in the cocoa.

3. Remove the saucepan from the heat and add the water and salt.

4. Stir and slowly add the sugar and vanilla. Cool before using.
Makes enough frosting for 6 muffins or cupcakes.

Lemon Glaze

1½ cups confectioners (powdered) sugar
½ cup lemon or lime juice
1 teaspoon vanilla extract

1. Place all ingredients in a large bowl and mix until smooth. The consistency will be slightly runny.

2. For best results, spread the glaze directly onto warm muffins, cakes or cookies.

3. Let the glaze harden before serving.
Makes enough glaze for 12 muffins or cupcakes.

Holiday Popcorn

There are several ways to make popcorn—with a popcorn machine, with a microwave, with prepackaged kernels in a container shaken over the stove, or by the traditional method. Choose the way that's easiest for you. Ask an adult to help you if you have never made popcorn before.

3 cups popcorn
3 tablespoons butter
1 tablespoon sugar
¼ teaspoon cinnamon
⅛ teaspoon nutmeg

1. Put the popcorn in an extra large bowl. Set the bowl aside.

2. Melt the butter in a small saucepan on the stove, over low heat. Turn the handle to one side.

3. Pour the butter over the popcorn and lightly toss it with 2 spoons so that the popcorn is coated with the butter.

4. Combine the sugar, cinnamon, and nutmeg in a small- to medium-sized bowl.

5. Sprinkle the sugar mixture over the popcorn. Toss the popcorn to coat it completely.

Makes about 3 cups popcorn.

Granola Bars

1¼ cup uncooked quick oats
½ cup raisins
½ cup peanuts
¼ cup coconut
⅓ cup melted butter
1 egg, beaten
½ teaspoon vanilla
⅓ cup packed brown sugar
½ teaspoon salt

1. Heat oven to 350 degrees F.

2. Grease well a 13-inch x 9-inch shallow baking pan or two 8-inch square baking pans.

3. Spread the oats in a shallow, ungreased baking sheet. Toast them in the oven for 15 to 20 minutes until light brown. Watch carefully so that they don't burn and turn black.

4. When the oats have been toasted, carefully spoon them into a large bowl. Use a large wooden spoon to combine the toasted oats with the rest of the ingredients. Mix well.

5. Pour the mixture into the prepared baking pan(s). Press the mixture down firmly.

6. Bake for 20 minutes. Cool for 30 minutes and cut into bars.
Makes 15 to 20 bars.

Special Cookie Paint

To make this paint, you must separate an egg. To learn how, see the instructions on page 99.

1 egg yolk
¼ teaspoon water
Assorted food colorings

1. In a small bowl, mix together the egg yolk and water until well blended.

2. Divide the mixture among several cups. Add a different food coloring to each cup. If the "paint" gets too thick, just add a few drops of water.

3. With small paintbrushes, paint designs on the cookies before you bake them.

Cookie Icing

2 tablespoons melted butter
2 cups confectioners (powdered) sugar
2 teaspoons vanilla extract
2 tablespoons milk
3–4 drops food coloring

1. With a large wooden spoon, mix together the butter, sugar, vanilla, milk, and food coloring in a medium-sized bowl.

2. Spread the frosting over the cookie, or dab it on for decoration.

Easy Fruit Cake

2 cups flour
1 cup white sugar
1 cup brown sugar
1 teaspoon baking soda
2 eggs
1 16-ounce can fruit cocktail with juice
½ cup chopped walnuts
¼ cup brown sugar

1. Heat oven to 325 degrees F.

2. Grease an 8-inch square baking pan.

3. Using a fork, mix together the flour, white and brown sugars, and baking soda in a large bowl.

4. Add the eggs and the fruit cocktail. Stir with a large spoon and pour the mixture into a baking pan. Use a rubber spatula to scrape the bowl.

5. Mix the walnuts and sugar in a separate, small bowl. Sprinkle the mixture on top of the batter.

6. Bake 70 minutes until a toothpick inserted in the center comes out clean. Cool in the pan for 45 minutes.

Makes 1 cake.

Apple Raisin Delight

1 large sour apple, such as a **Granny Smith** or **Macintosh**
2 tablespoons butter
1 tablespoon cornstarch
½ cup water
1 cup raisins
½ cup chopped walnuts
½ teaspoon cinnamon
¼ teaspoon cloves
¼ teaspoon nutmeg
⅓ cup brown sugar
⅛ teaspoon salt
Heavy cream, whipped cream, or vanilla ice cream (optional)
Walnuts or pecans (optional)

1. Wash the apple, cut it in half, and remove the core and seeds. Cut the halves into quarters, and then into bite-size pieces. Put the apple pieces aside for the moment.

2. Melt the butter in a medium-sized saucepan on the stove, over low heat.

3. Add the chopped apple pieces, and stir them in the hot butter until they are slightly browned.

4. Add the cornstarch, water, raisins, and walnuts. Stir, cooking slowly for 5 minutes over medium heat, until the mixture thickens.

5. Add the cinnamon, cloves, nutmeg, sugar, and salt. Cook until the sugar melts.

6. Let the mixture cool slightly before serving. Serve with cream, whipped cream, or vanilla ice cream. Sprinkle with walnuts or pecans, if you wish.

Makes 2 servings.

Ginger Plum Cake

1 16-ounce can of plums (or peaches or apricots)
1 package gingerbread mix
½ teaspoon salt
½ cup chopped walnuts or pecans
1 cup dark or golden raisins
Lemon Cream Icing (recipe follows) or whipped cream or
    vanilla ice cream

1. Heat oven to 375 degrees F.

2. Grease and flour an angel food cake pan (tube pan) or bundt pan.

3. Open the can of plums. Drain and save the plum juice or syrup, and chop up 1 cup of the plums.

4. In a large bowl, prepare the gingerbread mix according to the directions on the package. You may wish to substitute half of the liquid (water or milk) called for with the plum juice. Do NOT pour the mix into a baking pan or bake it yet.

5. To the gingerbread mixture, add the plums you chopped, the salt, nuts, and raisins.

6. Pour mixture into baking pan. Bake for 50 to 55 minutes, or until a toothpick inserted in the center comes out clean.

7. Let stand for 30 minutes to cool. Have an adult help you remove the cake from the pan—it's tricky.

8. Top with vanilla ice cream, whipped cream, or Lemon Cream Icing (recipe follows).

Makes 1 cake.

Lemon Cream Icing

¼ cup butter
½ cup sugar
2 tablespoons cornstarch
1 tablespoon milk
1 tablespoon lemon juice

1. Combine the butter, sugar, cornstarch, and milk in a small saucepan.

2. Place the saucepan on the stove over medium to medium-high heat, and stir the mixture constantly, until it boils. Then boil it for 1 minute.

3. Stir in the lemon juice.

4. Pour the hot icing over the ginger plum cake, and serve.
Makes enough icing to frost 1 cake.

Candy Cane Balls

10 small, round, hard, red-and-white peppermint candies
2 tablespoons sugar
2 drops red food coloring
2 drops green food coloring
2 scoops vanilla ice cream

1. Put the peppermint candies in a small plastic or paper bag, and ask an adult to help you crush them with a hammer. Be careful not to pound the candies too hard or the bag may break.

2. Put 1 tablespoon sugar and the red food coloring in a small bowl. Stir the sugar until the food coloring is mixed in. Add more food coloring, if desired.

3. In another small bowl, place the remaining tablespoon of sugar and the green food coloring. Stir the sugar until the food coloring is mixed in. Add more food coloring, if desired.

4. Using an ice cream scooper, place 1 scoop vanilla ice cream in each of two serving bowls.

5. Decorate each ice cream scoop with crushed peppermint candy bits and the colored sugars.

Makes 2 servings

© Christopher Bain 1988

Christmas Cookies You Can Decorate

⅓ cup honey
½ cup sugar
⅓ cup soft butter
1 egg
1 teaspoon vanilla extract
3 cups all-purpose flour
1 teaspoon baking soda

1 teaspoon salt
Special Cookie Paint (see page 106)
   OR
Raisins, red cinnamon candies, gumdrops, colored sugar, or sprinkles for decoration
Cookie Icing (see page 107)

1. In a large bowl, thoroughly mix together the honey, sugar, butter, egg, and vanilla extract.

2. In another bowl, mix together the flour, baking soda, and salt.

3. Next, mix ½ cup of the flour mixture into the butter mixture. Use a spatula to scrape the sides of the bowl. When the flour is mixed in, add another ½ cup and mix that in.

4. Repeat step 3 until all the flour and butter mixtures are in the same bowl and well blended. The cookie dough should be stiff.

5. Shape the dough into a ball, wrap it in plastic wrap, and chill it for 1 hour.

6. Heat the oven to 375 degrees.

7. Lightly grease a baking sheet.

8. Divide the dough into 3 portions. Return 2 of the portions to the refrigerator.

9. Place a little extra flour on your work surface and sprinkle some on your rolling pin. Then roll out the dough until it is about ⅛-inch thick. You can use a ruler to measure it.

10. Cut the dough into different shapes with cookie cutters.

11. Place the cookies on the baking sheet.

12. Repeat steps 9, 10, and 11 with the remaining dough.

13. Now the cookies are ready to decorate with the Special Cookie Paint or raisins, candies, or colored sugar. If you want to frost your cookies, you should do it after they are baked.

14. Bake the cookies for 6 to 8 minutes.

15. Then remove the baking sheet from the oven, and let the cookies cool on the sheet for about 2 minutes before removing them to a wire rack to cool completely.

Makes 60 cookies.

Gingerbread Boys

¼ cup butter
½ cup white or firmly packed brown sugar
½ cup dark molasses
¼ cup water
3 cups all-purpose flour
½ teaspoon salt

½ teaspoon baking powder
½ teaspoon powdered cloves
¾ teaspoon powdered ginger
¼ teaspoon nutmeg
½ teaspoon cinnamon
Raisins or cinnamon candies (optional)
Cookie Icing (see page 107)

1. In a large bowl, blend together the butter and sugar until creamy.

2. Add the molasses and sugar and mix well.

3. In another bowl, stir together the flour, salt, baking powder, cloves, ginger, nutmeg, and cinnamon.

4. Add ⅓ of the flour mixture to the molasses mixture and mix well. Add half of the remaining flour mixture and mix well again. Then add the rest and mix well again.

5. Form the dough into a ball and wrap it in plastic wrap.

6. Chill it in the refrigerator for at least an hour.

7. Heat oven to 350 degrees.

8. Lightly grease a baking sheet.

9. Divide dough into three portions. Put two of the portions back in the refrigerator, until you are ready to use them.

10. Roll out a portion of dough on a lightly floured board, with a lightly floured rolling pin. (If the flour does not stick to the pin, smear a few drops of vegetable oil on it first, then add the flour.) Roll the dough until it is very flat, about ⅛-inch thick. You can measure its thickness with a ruler. Cookies that are too thick may not hold together well after baking.

11. Cut the dough with a gingerbread boy cookie cutter that has been dipped in flour.

12. Repeat steps 10 and 11 with the remaining dough.

13. With a wide spatula, place the cookies on the prepared baking sheet. Decorate the cookies before baking with the cinnamon candies and raisins. You can make each gingerbread boy look different by bending its arms or legs a little; that way, one gingerbread boy can be running or waving to you, as he comes out of the oven.

14. Bake the cookies for 8 to 10 minutes.

15. Cool the cookies slightly, then remove them from the baking sheet and cool them on a wire rack. After the cookies are baked, you can decorate them with frosting.

Makes about 30 cookies.

Part III

Celebrating Christmas:

Favorite Stories and Carols

FAVORITE CHRISTMAS STORIES

THE TAILOR OF GLOUCESTER

BY BEATRIX POTTER

(abridged)

I.

Back in the days when gentlemen wore white powdered wigs and fine coats of silk and taffeta, there lived a tailor in the city of Gloucester. In the window of a little shop on Westgate Street, he sat cross-legged on a table, from morning till dark.

All day long while the light lasted, the tailor sewed and snipped. But although he sewed fine silk for his neighbors, he himself was very, very poor—a little old man in spectacles, with a pinched face, old crooked fingers, and a suit of threadbare clothes.

He cut his coats without wasting anything, and often remarked that the small snippets left on the table would only be good for making little vests for mice.

One bitter cold day near Christmas

© Cathy Christy O'Connor

time, the tailor began to make a coat. It was to be a special coat of cherry-colored, corded silk, embroidered with pansies and roses, with a cream-colored satin vest. The Mayor of Gloucester would be wearing it at his wedding on Christmas Day.

The tailor wanted this coat to be the most beautiful and perfect ever made. If the mayor were pleased with it, perhaps the tailor would be asked to make coats for other gentlemen as well.

The tailor worked and worked on the coat. He measured the silk and cut it and shaped it, and worked until the snowflakes came down against the window panes and shut out the light. By then, all the pieces of silk and satin lay cut out on the table.

There were pieces for the coat and vest, as well as for pockets, flaps, and cuffs; even the buttons were in order. The

tailor would stitch the buttonholes in a cherry-colored, twisted silk thread, called "twist." He had everything ready to sew the next morning—well, almost ready. All that was missing was a single skein of twist to stitch the last buttonhole.

That evening, the tailor came out of his shop, fastened the window, and locked the door. No one lived there at night but little brown mice. All the old houses in Gloucester had mice. There were little mouse staircases, secret trap doors, and passageways through which the mice made their way from house to house.

The tailor came out of his shop and shuffled home through the snow. He lived in only the kitchen of a small house, for that was all the tailor could afford to rent. His sole companion was his cat, Simpkin, who was very fond of catching mice.

"Meeow?" said Simpkin, as the tailor opened the door.

The tailor replied, "Simpkin, we shall make our fortune with the Mayor's coat, but right now I am worn out. Take these—my last four pennies—and go to the market. Buy a penny's worth of bread, a penny's worth of milk, and a penny's worth of sausages.

"And, oh, Simpkin," he added, "with the last penny, buy me a skein of cherry-colored twist. I must have the twist or I cannot finish the coat!"

Simpkin went out, and the tailor, feeling chilled, sat down by the fireplace and thought of the wonderful coat.

II.

A sound startled the tailor from his thoughts. From the dresser at the other side of the kitchen came little noises—"Tip tap, tip tap, tip tap tip!"

"Now what can that be?" asked the Tailor of Gloucester, jumping up from his chair. The dresser was covered with little china pots and bowls, willow-patterned plates, teacups, and mugs.

The tailor crossed the kitchen and stood beside the dresser, listening, and peering through his spectacles. Again, from under a teacup, came those funny little noises—"Tip tap, tip tap, tip tap tip!"

"This is very peculiar," said the Tailor of Gloucester, and he lifted up the teacup, which was upside down.

Out stepped a little lady mouse, and she made a curtsy to the tailor! Then she hopped down off the dresser and slipped beneath the paneling near the floor.

The tailor was headed back to his chair by the fire, when there came other little noises from the dresser. He went back and turned over another teacup, which was upside down. Out stepped a little gentleman mouse, who bowed to the tailor!

Then, from all over the dresser, came a chorus of little tappings—"Tip, tap, tip tap, tip tap tip!" And out from under teacups, bowls, and basins stepped more little mice, who hopped off the dresser and slipped under the panelling near the floor.

But the tailor was thinking too hard about the coat for the Mayor of Gloucester to pay much attention to the mice. "Twenty-one buttonholes of cherry-colored silk!" he exclaimed. "To be finished in four days' time."

Then the tailor had another thought: "Was I wise to entrust my last bit of money to Simpkin? Suppose he forgets the twist!" Then the tailor wondered if he should have let the mice loose—Simpkin had no doubt caught them himself to enjoy later.

But the tailor's thoughts soon turned back to his coat, and he began speaking of it out loud to himself. The little mice came out and listened as he spoke, taking note of the pattern planned for the wonderful coat. Then all at once they ran away, scurrying together through the passages beneath the floor. They squeaked and called to one another, as they ran from house to house. Not one mouse was left in the tailor's kitchen, when Simpkin came back from his errands.

Simpkin was in a bad mood, for he did not like the snow, and there was snow in his ears. Sniffing the kitchen for his supper, he immediately noticed there were no mice left on the dresser. "Hmmph!" he thought. He put down the bread, sausages, and milk—but he hid the other little parcel in a teapot on the dresser.

"Simpkin," said the tailor, "where is my twist?"

If Simpkin had been able to talk, he would have asked: "Where are my MICE?"

The tailor went sadly off to bed, while Simpkin spent the night searching through the kitchen for his mice.

All the next day the tailor was ill, and the next day, and the next. In his feverish dreams, he cried out, "No more twist!"

III.

On Christmas Eve, and very late at night, the moon rose over the roofs and chimneys of Gloucester. There were no lights on in any windows, and no sounds from any homes. The city was fast asleep under the snow.

And still Simpkin wanted his mice.

Now, it is said that in the hours between Christmas Eve and dawn on Christmas morning all beasts and animals can talk. That night, when the Cathedral clock struck twelve, Simpkin wandered out of the tailor's door and into the snowy street.

The sound of merry roosters singing Christmas rhymes was ringing through the air. Cats were dancing and singing in attics across the way. The sparrows sang of Christmas pies, and even the robins awoke from their sleep and began to sing.

All this merriment only annoyed Simpkin, who was hungry and looking for food. He wandered over to the tailor's

shop, where light was glowing from the window. Creeping up, he saw that the shop was lit with many tiny candles. There was a snippeting of scissors, and snappeting of thread, and little mouse voices were singing gaily.

"Mew! Mew!" interrupted Simpkin, and he scratched at the door. But the key was under the tailor's pillow, so he could not get in. The little mice only laughed and tried another tune—
"Three little mice sat down to spin;
Kitty passed by and she peeped in.
'What are you at, my fine little men?'
'Making coats for gentlemen.'
'Shall I come in and cut off your threads?'
'Oh, no, Miss Kitty, you'd bite off our
    heads!' "

"Mew! scratch! scratch!" scuffled Simpkin on the window sill. Inside, the little mice sprang up and barred the window shutters and shut out Simpkin. But through the nicks in the shutters Simpkin could hear the click of thimbles. At one point he heard them shout in little voices, "No more twist! No more twist!"

Simpkin turned away and went home, thinking about the mice and how they were helping the poor tailor. When he got home, Simpkin found the tailor without fever, sleeping peacefully.

Then Simpkin went on tip-toe and took a little parcel of silk out of the teapot. He felt quite ashamed of his badness, compared with those good little mice!

When the tailor awoke in the morning, the first thing he saw was a skein of cherry-colored twisted silk on his patchwork blanket, and beside his bed stood the repentant Simpkin!

The sun was shining on the snow as the tailor got up and dressed. He went out into the street, with Simpkin running before him. The starlings whistled on the chimney stacks, but they sang their own little noises, not the words they had sung in the night.

"Alas," said the tailor, "I have my twist but no more time. This is Christmas Day and the Mayor will be married at noon! He'll wonder why his cherry-colored coat is not finished."

He unlocked the door of the little shop on Westgate Street, and Simpkin ran in, as if expecting something. But there was no one there! Not even one little mouse!

The boards were swept clean; the little ends of thread and the little silk snippets were all tidied away.

But on the table—oh joy! The tailor gave a shout, for there—where he had left plain cuttings of silk—lay the most beautiful coat and embroidered satin vest that would ever be worn by a Mayor of Gloucester.

There were roses and pansies on the coat facings, and the vest was trimmed with poppies and cornflowers. Everything was finished, except for one single buttonhole; and on that buttonhole was pinned a scrap of paper with these words—in teeny weeny writing—"No More Twist."

There began the luck of the Tailor of Gloucester. He grew quite stout and quite rich. He made the most wonderful coats and vests for all the wealthy merchants of Gloucester, and for all the fine gentlemen living in the countryside nearby.

No one had ever seen such ruffles, or such embroidered cuffs and folds! But his buttonholes were the greatest triumph of all.

The stitches of those buttonholes were so neat—*so* neat—it was a wonder they could be stitched by an old man in spectacles, with crooked old fingers and a tailor's thimble. The stitches were so very small, in fact, they looked as if they had been made by little mice!

IS THERE A SANTA CLAUS?

(Edited and abridged)

It sometimes happens that people begin to wonder if the things they believe in are really true. One of these things is Santa Claus. Have you ever wondered if there really is a Santa Claus?

In 1908, a little girl in New York City was so curious about whether or not there was a Santa Claus, she wrote a letter to the local newspaper, the New York *Sun.* The girl, Virginia O'Hanlon, hoped that the people in charge of the newspaper might be able to answer her question. She wrote:

Dear Editor:

I am eight years old.

Some of my friends say there is no Santa Claus.

Papa says, "If you see it in the *Sun,* it's so."

Please tell me the truth, is there a Santa Claus?

Virginia O'Hanlon
115 West 95th Street

One of the New York *Sun's* editors, a man named Francis P. Church, wrote Virginia the following reply:

Virginia, your little friends are wrong. Unfortunately, we live in an age when people only believe in what they can see and understand.

Yes, Virginia, there is a Santa Claus. He exists as certainly as love and generosity and devotion exist. Alas! How dreary the world would be if there were no Santa Claus! It would be as dreary as if there were no Virginias.

Not believe in Santa Claus! You might as well not believe in fairies! You might get your papa to hire men to watch in all the chimneys on Christmas Eve to catch Santa Claus, but even if they did not see Santa Claus coming down, what would that prove? Nobody sees Santa Claus, but that is no sign there is no Santa Claus.

The most real things in the world are those that neither children nor men can see. Did you ever see fairies dancing on the lawn? Of course not, but that's no proof that they are not there. Nobody can conceive or imagine all the wonders there are in the world that we have never seen or never can see.

Only faith, imagination, poetry, love, and romance can help us see and appreciate the world's heavenly beauty and mystery. Is it all real? Ah, Virginia, in all this world there is nothing else real and eternal.

No Santa Claus! Thank God he lives, and he lives forever. A thousand years from now, Virginia, nay, ten times ten thousand years from now, he will continue to make glad the heart of childhood.

THE LEGEND OF BEFANA

M any, many years ago a woman named Befana lived by herself on a small country road. The woman led a simple life and never wondered what the next day might bring.

One evening, as Befana was sweeping her cottage, she suddenly stopped and listened. Outside, in the distance, she thought she heard a trumpet. She went over to the window and looked out.

Riding up the road were three magnificent men in flowing robes and turbans. They were preceded by a young page, who was blowing his trumpet to announce their way.

Befana could hardly believe her eyes.

Imagine such splendid, royal men riding up her little road! Their horses were as tall and proud as any horses could be; and by the bright-colored silks that made up the kings' robes, Befana guessed they came from the Orient, where she had heard such riches existed.

To her surprise, the kings rode right up to her house and stopped outside her door. Their golden gowns shimmered in the evening light, and the jewels on their crowns shone like stars.

"Come in, Your Highnesses," said Befana, curtsying.

"No thank you, good woman," said the first king. "We've been following a bright star that is leading us to a newborn King, who will be the Savior of all the people."

"But we seem to have lost our way," added the second king.

Befana looked puzzled. "I'm sorry, but I don't know how to help you," she said.

"Join us in our search," said the third king. "Come help us find Him. When we do, we will offer the Child gifts and rejoice in His birth."

Befana looked up the road, where the kings and page were headed. It was dark outside. She was tired and it was suppertime.

"Couldn't we go tomorrow?" she asked.

"No," said the kings. "We must not linger."

All Befana had to ride on was an old brown donkey, and he needed a good night's rest. Besides, she just was not ready to leave her cottage while it was in such disorder.

"Tomorrow," said Befana. "I promise I'll join you then. Tonight, I'd like to finish my sweeping."

The three kings said, "Very well, then. If you cannot come now, we must be on our way." With that, they got back on their horses and disappeared up the road and into the night.

Befana returned to her sweeping, and when she had finished, she sat down to a quiet dinner of grapes and barley cakes. She thought again of the three kings and of the Child they were seeking.

"It must be no ordinary Babe, if such important men are looking for him," she said to herself.

Befana did not sleep well that night. At the first light of dawn, she left her spotless cottage and headed up the road on her donkey, determined to find the three kings.

Befana rode and rode and asked everyone along the way if they had seen the three kings, or heard of the whereabouts of the newborn King. But everyone she asked just shook their heads, and Befana rode onward. She never returned to her cottage.

Years passed and Befana grew old. She realized that she might never find the Child and felt sorry that she had never seen Him or given Him any presents. To make up for that, she gathered little sweets and trinkets whenever she could and put them in a large bag. Befana wanted to give these treats secretly to every child in the land.

On the next anniversary of the three kings' visit to her cottage, Befana carried out her plan. On that twelfth night after Christmas, every door in every village miraculously stood open. No one awoke as Befana left her presents at each house. Befana went everywhere—up and down main roads and forgotten streets. She went quickly and quietly, until her work was done. As the sun crept up over the horizon, Befana felt sleepy, warm, and happier than ever before.

Hundreds of years have passed since then, but many children in Italy and Russia still await her visit. In that time, Befana has gotten to know many, many children. For the naughty ones, she leaves behind coal and stones, and hopes they will be better next year. But for all good children, Befana brings a special gift.

What Befana receives in return is the joy and love of giving, year after year.

© Cathy Christy O'Connor

Illustration by Thomas Nast

A VISIT FROM ST. NICHOLAS
(The Night Before Christmas)

BY CLEMENT CLARKE MOORE

Twas the night before Christmas, when all through the house
Not a creature was stirring, not even a mouse.
The stockings were hung by the chimney with care,
In hopes that St. Nicholas soon would be there.

The children were nestled all snug in their beds,
While visions of sugar plums danced in their heads;
And mamma in her kerchief, and I in my cap,
Had just settled our brains for a long winter's nap—
When out on the lawn there arose such a clatter,
I sprang from my bed to see what was the matter.
Away to the window I flew like a flash,
Tore open the shutters and threw up the sash.

The moon, on the breast of the new-fallen snow,
Gave a lustre of midday to objects below;
When what to my wondering eyes should appear,
But a miniature sleigh and eight tiny reindeer,
With a little old driver, so lively and quick
I knew in a moment it must be St. Nick.
More rapid than eagles his coursers they came,
And he whistled and shouted and called them by name:
"Now, Dasher! now, Dancer! now, Prancer and Vixen!
On, Comet! on, Cupid! on, Donder and Blitzen!
To the top of the porch, to the top of the wall!
Now dash away, dash away, dash away all!"
As dry leaves that before the wild hurricane fly,
When they meet with an obstacle, mount to the sky,
So, up to the house-top the courses they flew,
With a sleigh full of toys—and St. Nicholas too.

And then in a twinkling I heard on the roof
The prancing and pawing of each little hoof.
As I drew in my head and was turning around,
Down the chimney St. Nicholas came with a bound.
He was dressed all in fur from his head to his foot,
And his clothes were all tarnished with ashes and soot;
A bundle of toys he had flung on his back,
And he looked like a peddler just opening his pack.

Illustration by Thomas Nast

His eyes, how they twinkled! his dimples, how merry!
His cheeks were like roses, his nose like a cherry;
His droll little mouth was drawn up like a bow,
And the beard on his chin was as white as the snow.
The stump of a pipe he held tight in his teeth,
And the smoke, it encircled his head like a wreath.
He had a broad face, and a little round belly
That shook, when he laughed, like a bowl full of jelly.

He was chubby and plump—a right jolly old elf—
And I laughed when I saw him, in spite of myself.
A wink of his eye and a twist of his head
Soon gave me to know I had nothing to dread.
He spoke not a word, but went straight to his work,
And filled all the stockings; then turned with a jerk,
And laying his finger aside of his nose,
And giving a nod, up the chimney he rose.

He sprang to his sleigh, to his team gave a whistle,
And away they all flew like the down of a thistle;
But I heard him exclaim, ere he drove out of sight:
"Happy Christmas to all, and to all a good night!"

Illustration by Thomas Nast

A CHRISTMAS CAROL

BY CHARLES DICKENS

(abridged)

Part One:

Ebenezer Scrooge

Ebenezer Scrooge was a squeezing, wrenching, grasping, scraping, clutching, miserable old sinner! No heat could warm him, no cold could chill him, and no wind that blew was more bitter than he.

Scrooge's only friend had been an old, crabby man just like him. That man was his partner, Jacob Marley, but Marley had been as dead as a doornail for seven years. Scrooge was all alone, but he liked it that way.

One cold, bleak Christmas Eve afternoon, Scrooge sat in his office counting his money. In a dismal little room behind him, a poor clerk named Bob Cratchit was trying to warm his hands over the single candle that lit his desk. Suddenly, Scrooge's nephew, Fred, burst cheerily through the front door.

"A Merry Christmas, uncle!" Fred said.

"Bah!" said Scrooge. "Humbug!"

" 'Humbug?' Uncle, you don't mean that!"

"Yes, I do," said Scrooge—and he did. To him, every day was meant for making money. Christmas time, the season for spending money and extending human kindness, was sheer nonsense to Scrooge.

Still, Fred was not discouraged, and he invited his uncle to a Christmas party the following afternoon. That only angered Scrooge.

"Good afternoon!" he snapped, shooing Fred away.

"Merry Christmas, uncle!" Fred called brightly as he left, but Scrooge just slammed the door.

At closing time, Scrooge glanced up at his clerk, Bob Cratchit, who was tugging a thin, white shawl around his shoulders. Cratchit was too poor to buy himself a real coat.

"I suppose you want tomorrow off," said Scrooge with a scowl.

"Yes. Please, sir," said Cratchit. "It's only once a year, sir."

"All right," grumbled Scrooge, "but be here all the earlier the *next* morning."

The clerk promised he would and closed the door behind him.

That evening, as Scrooge was unlocking the door to his gloomy house, he noticed something strange about the knocker on the door. There, on the very same plain knocker that Scrooge had seen every day of his life was old Jacob Marley's face!

The face was not angry or ferocious. It just stared at Scrooge through its ghostly spectacles. Scrooge stared back, and the face disappeared.

"Bah! Humbug!" said Scrooge, and closed the door with a bang.

Part Two: *Marley's Ghost*

Scrooge went upstairs. The house was dark, but he did not mind, because keeping it dark was cheaper than lighting candles. Still, Scrooge was bothered by the memory of Marley's face upon the knocker. He closed his bedroom door and double-locked himself in, just to be safe. After putting on his night clothes, he settled into a chair near the fire to take his nightly bowl of gruel.

Suddenly, an old bell that hung in the room began to swing. Soon, it rang out loudly, as did every bell in the house. Then, to Scrooge's astonishment and dread, a clanking noise began, as if someone were dragging a heavy chain.

Scrooge trembled in his chair, as the clanking came up the stairs, straight towards his door, and then straight *through* the door! And a specter passed into the room before his eyes. As it did, the flame in the fireplace shot up, as if crying out, "I know him—it's Marley's ghost!"

It was Marley's face, all right. The same pigtail, waistcoat, and boots—yet his body was transparent and chains hung round about him.

"Hmmph!" said Scrooge, as bitter and cold as ever. "What do you want with me?"

"Much!" said the spirit. It was Marley's voice, no doubt about it.

"Who are you?" demanded Scrooge.

"In life, I was your partner, Jacob Marley," said the ghost, sitting down in a chair across from Scrooge. "But you don't believe in me, do you?"

"No, I don't," said Scrooge.

With that, Marley moaned loudly and rattled his chains.

Scrooge was horrified. "Mercy! Dreadful apparition, why do you trouble me?" he cried.

Marley spoke solemnly. "It is required of every living person to walk among friends and strangers, to be generous and kind," the ghost said. "Because I did not do this in life, I am condemned to do so in death. I can never stop and never rest. Many weary journeys lie before me."

"But why do you come to me?" asked Scrooge.

"Oh, blind man!" shouted Marley. "You, who have shunned as many of life's opportunities as I did! The same terrible fate awaits you, too. But I come here tonight to warn you that you have a chance of escaping this."

In his strange and shadowy voice, Marley told Scrooge that he would be haunted by Three Spirits. The first would come when the church bell tolled one o'clock. The second would come the next night at the same hour; and the third, at the last stroke of midnight on the next night.

"Look to see me no more!" said Marley. "And remember what has passed between us." With that, he disappeared.

Scrooge tried to say, "Humbug!", but stopped at the first syllable, suddenly exhausted. He fell into bed and was instantly fast asleep.

Part Three: *The First of the Three Spirits*

The room was pitch black when Scrooge awoke. Outside, the church bell tolled a deep, dull, melancholy one o'clock.

Instantly, light flashed into the room and a strange figure appeared at Scrooge's bedside. He was small and looked like a child—almost. His hair was white, as if with age, yet his skin was smooth as a flower petal. He held a branch of fresh, green holly in his hand, and on his head he wore a crown that gave off a bright, clear light. Scrooge cleared his throat.

"Are you the Spirit, sir, that I was told to expect?"

"I am! I am the Ghost of Christmas Past," said the figure.

"Long Past?" asked Scrooge.

"No. Your past. The things you will see with me are shadows of things that have

been. Come! Rise and walk with me!"

The Spirit walked onto the window ledge and held out his hand for Scrooge to follow.

"But I am a mortal, and liable to fall!" cried Scrooge.

"Touch my hand," said the Spirit.

Scrooge did so and suddenly the two stood in the middle of a city. By the looks of the shop windows, it was clearly Christmas time here, too. The Ghost stopped at a certain warehouse door and asked Scrooge if he knew where they were.

"Of course! I learned my trade here!" Scrooge exclaimed. As they went inside, Scrooge was amazed to see an old gentleman in a Welsh wig, who was sitting behind a desk so high, his head nearly touched the ceiling. "Why, it's old Fezziwig! Bless his heart, he's alive again!" cried Scrooge. He called to the man, but the Spirit shook his head.

"No one can see us," said the Ghost.

Old Fezziwig laid down his pen and looked up at the clock, as it chimed seven times. He rubbed his hands, adjusted his large waistcoat, laughed heartily, and called out in a rich, fat, jolly voice, "Yo ho, there! Ebenezer! Dick!"

A young Ebenezer Scrooge came briskly in, accompanied by his fellow apprentice.

"There's Dick Wilkins!" said Scrooge to the Ghost. "He was very much attached to me. Poor Dick! Dear, dear!"

"Yo ho! No more work tonight," said Fezziwig. "It's Christmas Eve, my boys! Let's clear away and make lots of room."

In a minute, the furniture was cleared away, the floor was swept and watered, the lamps were trimmed, fuel was heaped upon the fire; and the warehouse was as snug and warm and bright a ballroom as you would even want to see on a winter's night.

The fiddler came and went up to the lofty desk, which he quickly made into a lively, musical balcony. The guests arrived: the jolly Mrs. Fezziwig and her three lovable daughters; six young gentlemen; the housemaid and her cousin, the baker; the cook and her friend, and the milkman. Some were shy, some were bold, but as the music started up, away they all went! Twenty couples dancing at

once, never minding a wrong step here and a clumsy twirl there.

There were dances and more dances. There was cake, too, and a huge roast beef. There were mince pies and plenty of beer. But the high point of the evening came when Fezziwig and Mrs. Fezziwig stood up to dance. They were a first-rate couple, spinning 'round and 'round. Everyone cheered, and then joined in the dancing themselves.

The lovely, little ball broke up at eleven o'clock, with Fezziwig and his wife exchanging heartfelt Christmas wishes with their guests as they left.

"Imagine!" said the Ghost. "Such a small thing could make those silly folks so happy. Why, the old man spent but a few pounds on his party—does he deserve so much praise?"

"It isn't that," said Scrooge, as heated by the remark as young Ebenezer himself would have been. "The happiness old Fezziwig gave is as great as if it cost a fortune. I wish..."

"What?" asked the Spirit.

"It's nothing. I'd just like to say a word or two to my clerk right now. That's all," said Scrooge.

In a flash, the Spirit whisked the two of them off to a different scene. There was Ebenezer, older now, in the prime of his life. He sat beside a fair young girl, who was crying.

"You've changed," the girl was saying. "You fear the world too much, and all you want is money and gain. You could never love a poor girl like me. I only hope your money can comfort you in hard times, the way I would have."

Ebenezer started to protest, but the girl stopped him. "Goodbye, Ebenezer!" she said. "I'll always love the man you once were."

"Spirit! Remove me from this place!"

cried Scrooge. And suddenly Scrooge was in bed, in a deep, heavy sleep.

Part Four: *The Second of the Three Spirits*

When Scrooge awoke, his bedroom and the adjoining sitting room had undergone a surprising transformation. The walls were thick with holly, mistletoe, and ivy. A mighty blaze was roaring in the fireplace, and heaped upon the floor was an enormous feast. There were turkeys, geese, sausages, plum puddings, barrels of oysters, cherry-cheeked apples, cakes, and great bowls of punch.

On Scrooge's couch sat a Giant, glorious to see. He raised a glowing torch in his hand to shed its light on Scrooge, who peeked out from his bedroom door.

"Come in, come in!" urged the Giant. "I am the Ghost of Christmas Present."

Scrooge shuffled in, wearing slippers. "Lead me where you will, Spirit," he said. "Last night I learned a lesson that is working now. I am ready to learn from what you have to show me."

"Touch my robe!" said the Spirit.

Scrooge did as he was told, and the room and all its contents vanished. They stood in the city streets on a snowy Christmas morning. Invisible, the two went directly to Bob Cratchit's humble home.

In the kitchen, Mrs. Cratchit and young Belinda, Martha, and Peter Cratchit stood boiling, mashing, sweetening, and stirring the various dishes for the Christmas meal. Meanwhile, Bob Cratchit was seating one son, Tiny Tim, beside him at the corner of the table.

Poor Tiny Tim was crippled, and bore a little crutch. It was easy to see that Bob adored this son and had faith that he would grow to be strong and healthy.

When everything was hissing hot and ready to be served, the family gathered around the dining table. The Cratchits were not a handsome family; they were not well dressed; and they were poor. But none of that dimmed the excitement of sitting down with one another at Christmas dinner.

There was a breathless pause around the table, as Mrs. Cratchit raised the carving knife to cut the goose. When she did, and the gush of stuffing issued forth, a murmur of delight arose among all the Cratchits; even Tiny Tim feebly cried, "Hurrah!"

The goose was not large, but to the Cratchits, it was fit for a king; along with mashed potatoes and applesauce, it was enough dinner for the whole family.

The meal's grand finale, of course, was the plum pudding, a dessert of utmost importance to any Christmas dinner. To the Cratchits, the thought each year that the pudding would be less than perfect was enough to set each family member on the edge of his seat. But they should not have worried.

It was a wonderful pudding! It was round, like a speckled cannon ball, so hard and firm; it blazed in an eighth of an inch of brandy, with a sprig of Christmas holly stuck in the top. Everybody had something to say about the pudding, but nobody said or thought that it was a small pudding for a large family. Any Cratchit would have blushed to hint at such a thing.

After dinner, Bob Cratchit drew his family around the fireplace, a small glass of punch in his hand. He held the glass high and said, "A Merry Christmas to us all, my dears. God bless us!" And all the family echoed this sentiment.

"God bless us every one!" said Tiny Tim. He sat close to his father, upon his little stool. Bob took Tim's withered little hand in his, and held it as if he feared that the child would be taken from him.

"Another toast," said Bob, "to Mr. Scrooge, the Founder of the Feast!"

"The Founder of the Feast indeed!" cried Mrs. Cratchit, reddening. "If he were here, I'd give him a piece of my mind to feast upon!"

"My dear," said Bob, "the children! Christmas day."

Scrooge looked startled at hearing himself talked about that way. It disturbed him that his very name seemed to have cast a heavy shadow over the Cratchit family's merry afternoon. But when the gloom passed away, the family seemed ten times merrier than they had before.

The Cratchits were happy, grateful, and pleased with one another. They looked even happier in the bright sprinkling of the Spirit's torch at parting. Scrooge looked at all of them, especially Tiny Tim, until the happy scene faded from his sight.

In the distance, the church clock struck twelve. Scrooge looked about him and saw that the Ghost had disappeared. But lifting up his eyes, Scrooge saw a solemn Phantom, draped and hooded, coming toward him like a mist along the ground.

Part Five: The Last of the Spirits

The Phantom approached slowly, gravely, and silently. It was shrouded in a deep, black garment that concealed its head, face, and form. It left nothing visible save one outstretched hand. Scrooge knew nothing more of this gloomy, mysterious spirit, for it neither spoke nor moved.

"Am I in the presence of the Ghost of Christmas Yet to Come?" asked Scrooge, falling to his knees. "I fear you more than any specter I have seen so far. But I know your purpose is to do me good; since I hope to live a new life after this, I am prepared to join you now. And I do it with a thankful heart."

The Spirit gave no reply. The hand was pointed straight before them.

"Lead on, Spirit!" said Scrooge.

Quickly, they were in the heart of the city. The Spirit stopped beside a knot of businessmen and pointed to them. Scrooge went toward them to listen to their talk.

"When did he die?" asked one man.

"Last night, I believe," said another.

"Why, what was the matter with him?" asked a third.

"Who knows?" said the second man, with a yawn. "I thought he'd never die."

"And what did he do with his money?" asked the first.

The second man replied with a laugh, "All I know is—he didn't leave it to me!"

The men parted, chuckling among themselves.

Scrooge did not know what to think of the conversation. He was not quite sure who had died, and why the Spirit had wanted him to listen. But when the Spirit led him to his office and Scrooge did not see himself there, he began to understand.

When the Spirit took Scrooge past his house, Scrooge saw a cleaning woman and a laundress walking out with huge bundles over their backs. From their conversation, Scrooge realized that they had taken away his curtains, blankets, and best clothes in order to sell them.

"If he'd wanted to keep them after he was dead," said the cleaning woman, "why, he'd have had somebody to look after them, instead of dying sick and alone by himself."

"It's absolutely true," said the laundress. "He deserved what he got!"

Scrooge listened to this in horror. "Spirit," he cried, "please, let me see some tenderness connected with this death!"

The Ghost conducted him to poor Bob Cratchit's house, but the scene this time was very different from the merry one he had visited earlier. Bob, Mrs. Cratchit, Peter, Belinda, and Martha were seated around the fire. They were all quiet, very quiet.

Bob was reading aloud to them, trying to be pleasant and cheerful, but not succeeding at all. His eyes were brimming with tears, which he would dash away with the back of his hand.

Scrooge saw that the little stool next to

Bob was empty. On it lay a tiny crutch. "Tiny Tim!" Scrooge exclaimed. "Oh, no, not Tiny Tim!"

The Cratchit house suddenly faded and the air grew dark and still. The Ghost of Christmas Yet to Come led Scrooge to a dismal churchyard. The Spirit stood among the graves and pointed down to one.

"Oh, Spirit, before I look upon that stone, tell me that these are only shadows of things that Might be, not of things that Will be!"

The Ghost continued to point at the grave.

"Please, Spirit, tell me that if I change my life, its end will also change. Tell me that is why you have shown me these ter rible things!"

Still, the Ghost would not answer, and Scrooge crept toward the grave. The stone was marked, "Ebenezer Scrooge."

"Tell me it's not so, Spirit!" cried Scrooge. "I am not the man I was. I will honor Christmas in my heart and try to keep it all year through. I will live in the

Past, the Present, and the Future. I will not shut out the lessons the Spirits have taught me. Oh, tell me I may erase the writing on this stone!"

Scrooge held up his hands in one last prayer. As he did, the Phantom's hood and dress shrank, collapsed, and dwindled down into a bedpost.

And the bedpost was his own. The bed was his own, the room was his own. Best and happiest of all, the Time before him was his own. Scrooge was free to change his life and make it better.

Part Six:
Scrooge's Christmas

Scrooge ran to the window and opened it. Outside was a bright, stirring, golden day. The church bells were ringing out the lustiest peals he had ever heard.

"What's today?" cried Scrooge, calling down to a boy in Sunday clothes.

"Today? Why, *Christmas day!*" replied the boy.

"Hurray! I haven't missed it!" exclaimed Scrooge. With that, he offered the boy a silver dollar if he'd go down to the poultry store and buy the big prize turkey hanging in the window.

"Tell them to bring it here, so I can tell them where to take it," said Scrooge. The boy was off like a shot.

"I'll send it to Bob Cratchit's!" said Scrooge, tickled with pleasure, "and he'll never guess who sent it!"

Later that morning, Scrooge put on his best clothes and went out into the streets. People were everywhere, and Scrooge looked at everyone with a delightful smile. He looked so irresistibly pleasant that three or four good-natured fellows said, "Good morning, sir! A merry Christ-mas to you!" And Scrooge said often afterwards, that of all the beautiful sounds he had ever heard, those words were the most beautiful in his ears.

That afternoon, Scrooge surprised his nephew, Fred, by showing up at his house for dinner.

"Why bless my soul!" cried Fred, upon seeing his uncle—and it's a wonder Fred did not shake Scrooge's arm off. It was a wonderful party of close friends. They played games and sang happily all afternoon.

The next morning Scrooge could hardly conceal his new happiness. But he greeted Bob Cratchit in his usual severe manner.

"You're late, Cratchit!" he barked.

"I'm very sorry, sir. It won't happen again, sir," said Bob.

"Now, I won't stand for this any longer! And therefore," said Scrooge, laying a hand on Bob's shoulder—and "therefore, I am about to raise your salary!"

Bob trembled and looked up.

"A merry Christmas, Bob!" laughed Scrooge. "Yes, my friend, I'll raise your salary and try to help your struggling family. We'll discuss your affairs this very afternoon. So make up the fires, Bob, and buy a second bag of coal before you do another thing!"

Scrooge was better than his word. He did it all and much, much more. And to Tiny Tim, who did NOT die, he became a second father. Some people laughed to see the change in Scrooge, but his own heart laughed, and that was quite enough for him.

It was always said that if any man knew how to keep the Christmas spirit, Ebenezer Scrooge knew how. May that truly be said of all of us! And so, as Tiny Tim was fond of saying, "God Bless Us Every One!"

© Bob Kosturko 1988

THE LEGEND OF THE CAT

O n the night of the First Christmas, the beasts and birds quickly flocked to Bethlehem to honor the Baby Jesus. Among those visitors was the Cat. Unlike most of the animals, who were somewhat noisy in their eagerness to see the Child, the Cat came quietly, on her padded paws.

While the other animals pushed forward to look in the manger, the Cat stood back shyly. Nor could she kneel in praise, as the others did, for she was too awed by the sight to move at all. When the deer, lion, pheasant, rabbit, and fox burst into a hymn to Jesus, the Cat could only make a low, nervous tremble that caught in her throat.

As the sun rose in the morning, the animals returned home to the wild, one by one. Only the Cat remained in the stable. She continued to gaze upon the beautiful Nativity scene, unwilling to go back to her home in the forest.

Mary noticed how the Cat had stayed. She looked upon the animal's proud, serious face and smiled. "I bless you, Cat," she said. "From now on, you will never have to go back to the wilderness. Instead, wherever there are warm homes and caring people, you shall be there too."

Today, the gleam in a cat's eyes still speaks of her first life in the wild; her sharp claws and wild, lonely cry at night are other reminders of that time. But just feel a cat purr sweetly in your arms, or cuddle up against your leg—and you will think of Mary's blessing of the Cat on that very First Christmas.

THE LEGEND OF ROBIN RED- BREAST

© Cathy Christy O'Connor

On that First Christmas, it is said, the night was wrapped in a bitter chill. The small fire in the stable was nearly out, and the Mother Mary worried that her Baby would be cold. She turned to the animals about her and asked them for help.

"Could you blow on the embers," she asked the ox, "so the fire might continue to keep my Son warm?"

But the ox lay sound asleep on the stable floor and did not hear her.

Next, Mary asked the donkey to breathe life back into the fire, but the sleeping donkey did not hear Mary either. Nor did the horse or sheep. She wondered what to do.

Suddenly, Mary heard a fluttering of little wings. Looking up, she saw a plain, brown-colored robin fly into the stall. This robin had heard Mary calling to the animals and had come to help her himself. He went over to the dying fire and flapped his wings hard.

His wings were like little bellows, huffing and puffing air onto the embers, until they glowed bright red again. He continued to fan the fire, singing all the while, until the ashes began to kindle.

With his beak, the robin picked up some fresh, dry sticks and tossed them into the fire. As he did, a flame suddenly burst forth and burned the little bird's breast a bright red. But the robin simply continued to fan the fire until it crackled brightly and warmed the entire stable. The Baby Jesus slept happily.

Mary thanked and praised the robin for all he had done. She looked tenderly at his red breast, burned by the flame, and said, "From now on, let your red breast be a blessed reminder of your noble deed."

And to this day, the robin's red breast covers his humble heart.

THE NUTCRACKER

Adapted from "The Nutcracker and the King of the Mice"

BY E.T.A. HOFFMAN

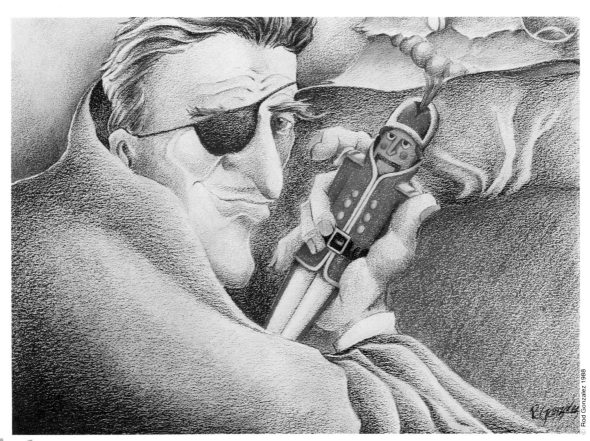

© Rod Gonzalez 1988

This story is the basis of a famous ballet set to the music of Peter Tchaikovsky. You may have seen this ballet around Christmas time, either on television or in a theatre. *The Nutcracker* is one of the world's most popular ballets.

Dr. Drosselmeyer's Surprise

It was Christmas Eve in a small, snow-covered town in Germany, many years ago. At the von Stahlbaums' home a party was in progress, and the air fairly crackled with the joy of friends and relatives gathered together. A fire blazed in the hearth; the banquet table was laden with delicious foods; and round about the Christmas tree, the children were eagerly unwrapping their presents.

"Look—toy soliders!" cried Fritz von Stahlbaum, and he held up a blue-jacketed soldier for all to admire.

Fritz's sister, Clara, opened her present next. "Ballet shoes!" she exclaimed. "These are just what I wanted!"

The other children were equally content with their presents, and the grownups stood by watching, pleased and amused.

Suddenly, a strong, cold burst of wind whipped down the front hall and into the parlor where everyone was gathered. Through the door came a mysterious-looking man in a powdered wig and a thick, black cloak. The room fell silent for a moment, and the children scurried to the protection of their parents.

But Mr. and Mrs. von Stahlbaum greeted their guest heartily. "Merry Christmas, Dr. Drosselmeyer! Come in!" they said, welcoming their friend and Clara's godfather.

Everyone knew that Dr. Drosselmeyer was no ordinary doctor. He wore a patch over one eye, like a pirate, and he moved his hands swiftly—like a magician.

Dr. Drosselmeyer smiled and bowed to his hosts; he then waved to two footmen, who brought in a pair of dolls—a boy and a girl, dressed as clowns. He wound the dolls up and they sprang into a dance so lively, they seemed almost real.

"More! More!" cried the children, forgetting their fear of the doctor.

Dr. Drosselmeyer drew the children into a circle around him. From the depths of his thick, black cape he pulled out a large, wooden Nutcracker, carved and brightly painted to resemble a soldier. His jacket was scarlet, like the jaunty feather in his helmet, and he had a stiff smile on his face.

A dozen eager hands shot up at once, each child hoping to receive this beautiful toy. Dr. Drosselmeyer reached over their heads and handed the Nutcracker to Clara.

"For me?" she exclaimed, astonished to receive a second wonderful gift. She cradled the Nutcracker in her arms.

Fritz eyed his sister enviously. "Let *me* see it," he said, grabbing it out of her hands. Fritz turned and ran with it, when suddenly he tripped and fell, smacking the Nutcracker against the floor. The lovely toy lay broken and Clara burst into tears.

The evening ended shortly afterward, as tears were dried and apologies given. Before he left, Dr. Drosselmeyer picked the Nutcracker up and placed it gently under the tree. The last remaining guest went home, yawning happily, and the lights were put out one by one. Fritz and Clara were tucked into bed, and soon the whole house was fast asleep.

II. The Nutcracker and The Seven-Headed Mouse

Clara awoke in the middle of the night. She wondered where her Nutcracker was and crept out of bed to find it. The house was dark and full of shadows, as Clara stole silently downstairs to the parlor door. Peeking in, she was relieved to see the Nutcracker lying safely under the tree.

Clara wanted to take the Nutcracker upstairs with her, but the parlor felt spooky in the night; the curtains fluttered and made strange patterns on the wall, and the floorboards creaked eerily. At last, Clara took a deep breath and entered the room. Suddenly, there was a whirring noise and the owl on the grandfather clock flapped its wings. Clara gasped and fell to the floor, covering her face, while the clock struck twelve o'clock.

As Clara lay on the floor, two grey mice came running out of the shadows. They sniffed at her, then ran away. When the room was quiet again, Clara scrambled to

her feet and ran to the Christmas tree. Just then, a large shadow—shaped like Dr. Drosselmeyer's cloak—fell across the room. Clara froze, not knowing what to do.

In another second, the shadow vanished and the most amazing thing happened: the Nutcracker, magically mended, came to life! He sprang to his feet and bowed to Clara, who curtsied politely back at him.

But there was no more time for introductions, for an army of great gray mice was pouring into the parlor. They were led by the Mouse King—a ferocious mouse with seven heads. The Nutcracker quickly called his own troops together, and Fritz's toy soldiers came marching into battle. Rifles flared and swords flashed, as the two armies met. Clara watched anxiously from the corner of the room. Many mice and toy soldiers were falling, wounded, to the floor. Before long, the Mouse King and the Nutcracker came face-to-face.

Clash! Clash! went the two leaders' swords. The Nutcracker fought bravely, but the Mouse King was too strong and too sly for him.

"Watch out!" cried Clara, as she watched the Mouse King run up to attack the Nutcracker from behind. Alarmed, she picked up one of her ballet slippers and threw it as hard as she could at the terrible, seven-headed mouse. The slipper hit the mouse in one of his faces, and the Mouse King was stunned. The Nutcracker quickly seized that moment to make his final charge.

The Mouse King fell dead to the ground, and the other mice soldiers fled. The Nutcracker and his soldiers were victorious!

Clara cheered. The Nutcracker stooped to pick up the ballet slipper and when he arose, he was no longer a wooden soldier. Instead, the Nutcracker had turned into a real, live Prince.

Still holding the slipper, the Prince walked over to Clara and dropped to one knee before her. "Thank you for saving my life," he said. The Prince then took the crown off the Mouse King and placed it on Clara's head. "I crown you Princess Clara," he said. "Please come and be my guest in the Kingdom of Sweets."

"Thank you!" said Clara.

With that, the two joined hands and began their journey.

III. The Land of Snow

With a royal sweep of his arm, the Prince cast the parlor walls away, and he and Clara stood in the midst of a beautiful winter wonderland. All about them were gentle snowbanks and fir trees. Falling snowflakes sparkled in the moonlight.

Little snowflake fairies circled about Clara to welcome her. When they melted away, more fairies appeared to dance around their visitor. Clara ran happily among them, while the air filled with lovely, light music—like fairy voices singing from the trees.

An elegant carriage made of half a walnut arrived to take Clara and the Prince to the Kingdom of Sweets. They climbed in and waved farewell to the Land of Snow. The silver-white fairies twirled and floated about them until the two were out of sight.

IV. The Kingdom of Sweets

Clara could hardly believe her eyes, as she and the Prince entered the enchanted kingdom. The palace walls were made of enormous, jelly-like blocks of Turkish delight, and the archways of marshmallows. The main entrance was adorned with carvings made from caramel and toffee, and enormous vases were filled with lemon custard and chocolate pudding.

The Sugar Plum Fairy, who ruled the Kingdom of Sweets, came fluttering down from her throne. She wore a pink, silk robe that was covered in delicate, crystallized sugar, as dainty as lace; on her head was a coronet of stars, which sparkled as she moved.

With a wave of the Sugar Plum Fairy's wand, a cook appeared behind a magical kitchen stove. Then more cooks appeared, stirring and whipping up all kinds of concoctions in large bowls. With another wave of her wand, several kitchen maids appeared and began to set a large table.

"How do you do, Princess Clara?" asked the Sugar Plum Fairy. "The Kingdom of Sweets is preparing a feast in your honor, because you saved our Prince's life. Please have a seat at the royal table."

Eyes wide with delight, Clara sat at the head of the table and was treated to the most delicious dishes in all the land. Later, the Sugar Plum Fairy led Clara to her throne to watch the entertainment the kingdom's Sweets had prepared.

Clara had never seen such dancing before. "I didn't know *candies* could dance!" she exclaimed.

And yet there they were—funny, lively sweets—dancing! It was almost as if they were real people! First, the milk and dark chocolates did a fiery Spanish dance. Then three little marzipan shepherdesses stepped forward, skipping lightly while playing a song on their pipes. An agile pair of coffee-flavored sweets, dressed in Arabian silks, did remarkable acrobatics.

But the most amazing sight of all was that of a giant lady bonbon, named Mother Ginger, who was dressed in a full, elegant hooped skirt. When she lifted her skirt, out tumbled dozens of smaller, brightly wrapped "candies" that looked just like laughing, dancing children.

The highpoint of the evening was the Sugar Plum Fairy's own dance. It was a delight to watch the royal fairy twirl and spin and leap across the palace floor, for she was as light and graceful as spun sugar. The Fairy was then joined by her own prince, the Cavalier, who held her hand as she did beautiful little turns on the points of her toes. The Sugar Plum Fairy danced so lightly and easily, it seemed she might float away.

"She really *is* magic!" Clara thought to herself.

Clara wished she could stay in this land forever, but as dawn broke in the Kingdom of Sweets, she knew it was time to say goodbye. It was Christmas morning, and her family would be wondering where she was.

The Nutcracker Prince escorted Clara to the walnut carriage, which would take her home. The Prince kissed Clara lightly on the cheek and Clara smiled back at him.

As the carriage pulled away, the Sugar Plum Fairy, the cooks, kitchen maids, and all the Sweets waved goodbye to Princess Clara.

"Goodbye!" Clara called back. As she left, Clara was quite sure this wonderful adventure was the best Christmas gift she had ever received.

North Wind Picture Archives

FAVORITE CHRISTMAS CAROLS

WE WISH YOU A MERRY CHRISTMAS

Text and Tune: Traditional English

We wish you a merry Christmas,
We wish you a merry Christmas,
We wish you a merry Christmas,
And a Happy New Year!

Good tidings we bring,
To you and your kin.
We wish you a merry Christmas,
And a Happy New Year!

We all want some figgy pudding,
We all want some figgy pudding,
We all want some figgy pudding,
So bring it right here!

GOOD KING WENCESLAS

J.M. Neale, translator from the Latin

Good King Wenceslas looked out
On the Feast of Stephen,
When the snow lay round about,
Deep and crisp, and even:
Brightly shone the moon that night,
Though the frost was cruel,
When a poor man came in sight,
Gath'ring winter fuel.

"Hither, page, and stand by me,
If thou know'st it; telling,
Yonder peasant, who is he?
Where and what his dwelling?"
"Sire, he lives a good league hence,
Underneath the mountain;
Right against the forest fence,
By Saint Agnes' fountain."

"Bring me flesh and bring me wine,
Bring me pinelogs hither;
Thou and I will see him dine,
When we bear them thither,"
Page and monarch forth they went,
Forth they went together;
Through the rude wind's wild lament,
And the bitter weather.

"Sire, the night is darker now,
And the wind blows stronger;
Fails my heart, I know not how,
I can go no longer,"
"Mark my footsteps, my good page,
Tread thou in them boldly:
Thou shalt find the winter's rage,
Freeze thy blood less coldly."

In his master's steps he trod,
Where the snow lay dinted;
Heat was in the very sod
Which the saint had printed.
Therefore, Christian men, be sure,
Wealth or rank possessing,
"Ye who now will bless the poor,
Shall yourselves find blessing."

JOY TO THE WORLD

Text: Isaac Watts, 1719

Tune: Adapted from George F. Handel, 1742

Joy to the World!
The Lord is come;
Let earth receive her King;
Let every heart
Prepare Him room,
And heav'n and nature sing,
And heav'n and nature sing,
And heav'n and heav'n
And nature sing.

Joy to the world!
The Savior reigns;
Let men their songs employ,
While fields and floods,
Rocks, hills, and plains
Repeat the sounding joy,
Repeat the sounding joy,
Repeat, repeat
The sounding joy.

THE TWELVE DAYS OF CHRISTMAS

Text and Tune: Traditional English

On the first day of Christmas my true
    love gave to me
A partridge in a pear tree.

On the second day of Christmas my true
    love gave to me
Two turtle doves, and a partridge in a
    pear tree.

On the third day of Christmas my true
    love gave to me
Three French hens, two turtle doves, and
    a partridge in a pear tree.

On the fourth day of Christmas my true
    love gave to me
Four calling birds, three French hens, two
    turtle doves, and a partridge in a pear
    tree.

On the fifth day of Christmas my true
    love gave to me
FIVE GOLDEN RINGS, four calling birds,
    three French hens, two turtle doves,
    and a partridge in a pear tree.

On the sixth . . . Six geese a-laying, (repeat
    previous ones)

On the seventh . . . Seven swans a-
    swimming, (repeat)

On the eighth . . . . Eight maids a-milking,
    (repeat)

On the ninth . . . . Nine ladies dancing,
    (repeat)

On the tenth . . . . Ten lords a-leaping,
    (repeat)

On the eleventh . . . . Eleven pipers piping,
    (repeat)

On the twelfth . . . . Twelve drummers
    drumming, (repeat)

HARK! THE HERALD ANGELS SING

Text: Charles Wesley, 1739   **Tune: Felix Mendelssohn, 1840**

Hark! the herald angels sing,
Glory to the newborn King;
Peace on earth, and mercy mild,
God and sinners reconciled!
Joyful all ye nations rise,
Join the triumph of the skies;
With th'angelic host proclaim,
Christ is born in Bethlehem.

REFRAIN:
Hark! the herald angels sing,
Glory to the newborn King.

Christ, by highest heaven adored,
Christ, the everlasting Lord,
Late in time behold him come,
Offspring of a Virgin's womb.
Veiled in flesh the Godhead see!
Hail, the incarnate Deity!
Pleased as Man with man to dwell,
Jesus, our Emmanuel

(Refrain)

Hail, the heaven-born Prince of Peace!
Hail, the Sun of Righteousness!
Light and life to all he brings,
Risen with healing in his wings.
Mild he lays his glory by,
Born that man no more may die,
Born to raise the sons of earth,
Born to give them second birth.

(Refrain)

DECK THE HALLS

Text and Tune: Traditional Welsh

Deck the halls with boughs of holly,
Fa la la la la, la la la la;
'Tis the season to be jolly,
Fa la la la la, la la la la.
Don we now our gay apparel,
Fa la la, la la la, la la la.
Troll the ancient Yuletide carol
Fa la la la la, la la la la.

See the blazing Yule before us,
Fa la la la la, la la la la.
Strike the harp and join the chorus,
Fa la la la la, la la la la.
Follow me in merry measure,
Fa la la, la la la, la la la.
While I tell of Yuletide treasure,
Fa la la la la, la la la la.

Away In A Manger

Text: Anonymous   Tune: J.R. Murray, 1877

Away in a manger, no crib for a bed,
The little Lord Jesus laid down His sweet
    head.
The stars in the bright sky looked down
    where He lay,
The little Lord Jesus asleep on the hay.

The cattle are lowing, the Baby awakes,
But little Lord Jesus, no crying He makes.
I love thee, Lord Jesus, look down from
    the sky,
And stay by my cradle 'til morning is
    nigh.

We Three Kings

Text and Tune: John H. Hopkins, 1857

We three kings of Orient are;
Bearing gifts, we traverse afar,
Field and fountain, moor and mountain,
Following yonder star.

REFRAIN:

O-oh! Star of wonder, star of night,
Star with royal beauty bright;
Westward leading, still proceeding,
Guide us to Thy perfect light.

Born a King on Bethlehem's plain,
Gold I bring to crown Him again,
King forever, ceasing never,
Over us all to reign.

(Refrain)

O Little Town Of Bethlehem

Text: Philips Brooks   Tune: Lewis H. Redner

O little town of Bethlehem,
How still we see thee lie!
Above thy deep and dreamless sleep
The silent stars go by;
Yet in thy dark streets shineth
The everlasting Light;
The hopes and fears of all the years
Are met in thee tonight.

For Christ is born of Mary,
And gathered all above,
While mortals sleep, the angels keep
Their watch of wond'ring love.
O morning stars together
Proclaim the holy birth,
And praises sing to God the King,
And peace to men on earth!

O Christmas Tree!/ "O Tannenbaum!"

(Original in German)   Text and Tune: Traditional German

O Christmas tree, O Christmas tree!
With faithful leaves unchanging;
Not only green in summer's heat,
But also winter's snow and sleet.
O Christmas tree, O Christmas tree!
With faithful leaves unchanging.

"O Tannenbaum, O Tannenbaum!
Wie treu sind deine Blätter!
Du grünst nicht nur in Sommerzeit,
Nein, auch im Winter, wenn es schneit.
O Tannenbaum, O Tannenbaum!
Wie treu sind deine Blätter!"

Jingle Bells

Text and Tune: James Pierpont

Dashing through the snow
In a one-horse open sleigh,
O'er the fields we go
Laughing all the way;
Bells on bobtails ring,
Making spirits bright;
What fun it is to laugh and sing
A sleighing song tonight—Oh!

Jingle bells, jingle bells,
Jingle all the way!
Oh, what fun it is to ride
In a one-horse open sleigh!
Jingle bells, jingle bells,
Jingle all the way!
Oh, what fun it is to ride
In a one-horse open sleigh!

Bring A Torch, Jeannette, Isabella/
"Un Flambeau, Jeannette, Isabelle"

(Original in French)   Translation: E. Luthbert Nunn
Text: Traditional Provençal, 17th Century   Tune: 17th Century Provençal Carol

Bring a torch, Jeannette, Isabella,
Bring a torch to the cradle run!
It is Jesus, good folk of the village;
Christ is born and Mary's calling:
Ah! Ah! beautiful is the Mother,
Ah! Ah! beautiful is her Son!

"Un flambeau, Jeannette, Isabelle,
Un flambeau, courons au berceau!
C'est Jésus, bonnes gens du hameau,
Le Christ est né, Marie appelle,
Ah! Ah! que la mère est belle,
Ah! Ah! que l'Enfant est beau!"

Robert Grav

SILENT NIGHT, HOLY NIGHT/
"STILLE NACHT, HEILIGE NACHT"

(Original in German)

Text: Joseph Mohr, 1818   Tune: Franz Gruber, 1818   Translation: John F. Young, 1871

Silent night, Holy night;
All is calm, all is bright;
Round yon virgin Mother and Child.
Holy Infant so tender and mild,
Sleep in heavenly peace,
Sleep in heavenly peace.

Silent night, Holy night;
Shepherds quake at the sight;
Glories stream from heaven afar,
Heavenly hosts sing alleluia.
Christ, the Savior is born!
Christ, the Savior is born!

"Stille Nacht, Heilige Nacht;
All' schläft, einsam wacht,
Nur das traute hoch heilige Paar.
Holder Knabe im lockigen Haar,
Schlaf in himmlischer Ruh,
Schlaf in himmlischer Ruh."

O COME, ALL YE FAITHFUL/
"ADESTE FIDELIS"

Text and Tune: John Wade, c. 1740   (Original in Latin)   Translation: Frederick Oakley, 1841

O come, all ye faithful,
Joyful and triumphant,
O come, ye; O come ye,
To Bethlehem.
Come and behold Him,
Born the King of Angels;

Sing, choirs of angels,
Sing in exultation,
Sing all ye citizens of heav'n above!
Glory to God, all glory in the highest!

(Refrain) (Cont'd., in Latin)

"Adeste fideles, Laeti triumphantes,
Venite, venite in Bethlehem!
Natum videte,
Regem angelorum;
Venite adoremus,
Venite adoremus,
Venite adoremus,
Dominum!"

REFRAIN:

O come, let us adore Him,
O come, let us adore Him,
O come, let us adore Him,
Christ, the Lord!

METRIC CONVERSIONS

Use the table of measures below to convert from metric to U.S. measures and vice versa. All conversions are approximate.

DRY WEIGHT MEASURES

25 grams	1 ounce	1 tablespoon
55 grams	2 ounces	¼ cup
85 grams	3 ounces	⅓ cup
110 grams	4 ounces	½ cup
170 grams	6 ounces	¾ cup
225 grams	8 ounces	1 cup
280 grams	10 ounces	1¼ cup
340 grams	12 ounces	1½ cup
450 grams	1 pound	2 cups
560 grams	1 pound, 4 ounces	2½ cups
675 grams	1½ pounds	3 cups

LIQUID MEASURES

30 milliliters	1 fluid ounce	⅛ cup
55 milliliters	2 fluid ounces	¼ cup
85 milliliters	3 fluid ounces	¾ cup
250 milliliters	11 fluid ounces	1 cup
340 milliliters	12 fluid ounces	1½ cups
450 milliliters	16 fluid ounces	2 cups
785 milliliters	28 fluid ounces	2¼ cups
1 liter	34 fluid ounces	1¾ pints

OVEN TEMPERATURES

300°F	150°C	Gas Mark 2
325°F	160°C	Gas Mark 3
350°F	180°C	Gas Mark 4
375°F	190°C	Gas Mark 5
400°F	200°C	Gas Mark 6

LENGTH

½ centimeter	⅛ inch
1 centimeter	¼ inch
2½ centimeters	1 inch
5 centimeters	2 inches
10 centimeters	4 inches
20 centimeters	8 inches

INDEX

U

United States
    Christmas seals in, 32–33
    Christmas tree tradition in, 26
    luminarias as tradition in, 29
Utensils, cooking, 96

V

Virgin Mary. *See* Mary
"Visit from St. Nicholas, A" (The
    Night Before Christmas)
    (Moore), 126–128

W

Wade, John, 152
Washington, D.C., Christmas tree
    in, 28
Wassail, meaning of, 36
Wastebaskets, decoration of, 60
Watts, Isaac, 147
"We Three Kings" (Hopkins), 149
"We Wish You a Merry Christmas,"
    145
Wenceslas. *See* Good King
    Wenceslas

Wesley, Charles, 148
White House (Washington, D.C.),
    Christmas tree in, 28
White sugar, 98
Windows, candles in, 29
Winter, pre-Christian era festivals
    during, 20
Wreaths, Advent, 29
Wyeth, N.C., *44*

Y

Young, John F., 152
Yule, meaning of word, 36
Yule log, tradition surrounding, 36